# Transfusion Medicine's Emerging Positions: Transfusion Safety Officers and Patient Blood Management Coordinators

Other related publications available from the AABB:

**Guidelines for the Quality Assessment of Transfusion**
By Jeffrey Wagner, BSN, RN;
James P. AuBuchon, MD, FCAP, FRCP(Edin);
Sunita Saxena, MD, MHA; and Ira A. Shulman, MD, FCAP
for the Clinical Transfusion Medicine Committee

**Guidelines for Patient Blood Management and Blood Utilization**
By Joanne Becker, MD, and Beth Shaz, MD for the
Clinical Transfusion Medicine Committee and the
Transfusion Medicine Section Coordinating Committee

**The Transfusion Commitee: Putting Patient Safety First,
2nd edition**
Edited by Sunita Saxena, MD, MHA

The AABB Press produces hard copy and electronic publications on many topics of interest to those in the blood banking, transfusion medicine, and cellular therapy fields.

To purchase books or to inquire about other book services, including digital downloads and large-quantity sales, please contact our sales department:
- 866.222.2498 (within the United States)
- +1 301.215.6499 (outside the United States)
- +1 301.951.7150 (fax)
- www.aabb.org>Resources>Marketplace

AABB customer service representatives are available by telephone from 8:30 am to 5:00 pm ET, Monday through Friday, excluding holidays.

# Transfusion Medicine's Emerging Positions: Transfusion Safety Officers and Patient Blood Management Coordinators

Editors

**Kathleen E. Puca, MD, MT(ASCP)SBB**
BloodCenter of Wisconsin
Milwaukee, Wisconsin

**Susan T. Johnson, MSTM, MT(ASCP)SBB**
BloodCenter of Wisconsin
Milwaukee, Wisconsin

AABB Press
Bethesda, Maryland
2013

AABB
8101 Glenbrook Road
Bethesda, Maryland 20814-2749

ISBN NO. 978-1-56395-870-0
Printed in the United States

**Library of Congress Cataloging-in-Publication Data**

Transfusion medicine's emerging positions : transfusion safety officers and patient blood management coordinators / editors, Kathleen E. Puca, Susan T. Johnson.
    p. ; cm.
Includes bibliographical references and index.
ISBN 978-1-56395-870-0
I. Puca, Kathleen E., editor of compilation. II. Johnson, Susan T., editor of compilation. III. AABB, publisher.
    [DNLM: 1. Blood Transfusion—trends. 2. Administrative Personnel—trends. 3. Blood Safety—trends. 4. Safety Management—organization & administration. 5. Safety Management—trends. WB 356]
    RM172
    362.17'84—dc23
                                                                    2013038031

# Contributors

**Julie DeLisle, RN, MSN**
BloodCenter of Wisconsin
Milwaukee, Wisconsin

**Shelley Feenstra, RN**
Vancouver Coastal Health
Vancouver, British Columbia

**Nanci Fredrich, RN, BSN, MM**
BloodCenter of Wisconsin
Milwaukee, Wisconsin

**Carole Ann LaGrange, MLT**
Alberta Health Services
Red Deer, Alberta, Canada

**Kimberly J. Maynard,
BSN, RN, OCN**
Dartmouth-Hitchcock
Medical Center
Lebanon, New Hampshire

**Colleen McGuinness Slapak,
MS, MT(ASCP)SBB**
Community Blood Center/
Community Tissue Services
Dayton, Ohio

**Houston Nguyen, MT(ASCP)**
Blood Systems, Inc.
Scottsdale, Arizona

**Joseph Thomas, RN, BSN**
Strategic Healthcare Group LLC
Indianapolis, Indiana

**Mary Townsend, MD**
Blood Systems, Inc.
Scottsdale, Arizona

**Jeffrey Wagner, BSN, RN**
Seattle, Washington

# Table of Contents

# Preface

 HOSPITALS TODAY ARE BEING CHALLENGED TO IM-
prove patient safety and outcomes while reducing costs.
Overuse or inappropriate use of blood components can
present significant patient safety issues and raise the cost of
care. Appropriate and safe transfusion therapy is a complex,
interlinking chain of events that depends on the integration and coordination among multiple hospital services, including physicians, laboratory medicine, nursing, pharmacy, anesthesia, surgery, and quality management. Not surprisingly, many institutions struggle with multiple
facets within this spectrum of care—given that no one individual or department oversees the entire process of transfusion practice.

A growing number of reports in the literature have suggested a
transfusion safety officer (TSO) or patient blood management coordinator (PBMC) as a position that can aid in improving patient care and optimize appropriate use of blood components. Countries such as Canada, France, and the United Kingdom have led the way in using TSOs
to reduce transfusion errors. Many health-care professionals are interested in promoting PBM and transfusion safety, but lack the knowledge
to develop a TSO or PBMC role as either a hospital-based or blood-center-based position. In addition, health-care workers may find themselves
alone in this newly created position at their institutions with little experience or resources to guide them in their new duties and responsibilities.

This book is intended to provide the interested reader with the history, current, and evolving roles of TSOs and PBMCs, as well as tools
and guidance for establishing a TSO or PBMC position. The contents
provide a template and guidance for building a business case. Over a
dozen job descriptions from colleagues across the country are provided
on the accompanying CD-ROM. Finally, information to aid in maximiz-
ing the performance and effectiveness of such a candidate is included.

It must be noted, however, responsibilities of a TSO or PBMC vary
widely, because this area of interest is still in its infancy. As a reflection

of the evolving landscape, chapters in this book offer different perspectives on the terminology, activities, and concerns of TSOs and PBMCs. The authors speak from their own experience gained "in the trenches" and from networking with colleagues around the world. Their goal of this book is to provide assistance to, and options for consideration by, readers who are preparing themselves for the future and moving their facilities forward. In addition, the chapter authors hope this book will serve as a reference for those who may find themselves in this new role as it gains wider acceptance in health-care institutions.

In researching for this book, there was limited printed material on these emerging positions in the field of transfusion medicine, particularly in the United States. Information presented in some of the chapters is based on the author's personal experience or communication with colleagues. Undoubtedly there have been several nurses, medical laboratory scientists, and other health-care professionals across the country who have been performing the duties of a TSO or PBMC for years, although without the formal title. Their efforts do not go unnoticed by the editors, and we apologize if there are inadvertent omissions of information about the development of these new roles in hospitals and blood centers. The editors invite feedback and suggestions on how to improve future editions.

The editors would like to thank all of the pioneers in this field—both the silent health-care workers who are at the patient's bedside as advocates for ensuring "the right product to the right patient for the right reason at the right time" and the more visible individuals who have advanced research in transfusion therapy and provided limitless publications for the education and training of TSOs, PBMCs, and transfusion medicine specialists alike.

Foremost, the editors extend heartfelt thanks to the chapter authors for taking time to share their expertise with others. Their energy and efforts in the face of declining available time for such educational pursuits is evident by the quality of the chapters put forth. We all owe a debt of gratitude to their employers, who can be called "early adopters" of this growing approach to improving patient care. The editors also appreciate the support of AABB and the Press Editorial Board members for giving us the opportunity to undertake this endeavor. Our special thanks to AABB Publications staff for their patience and assistance; without their help and guidance this book would not have been possible.

Kathleen E. Puca, MD, MT(ASCP)SBB
Susan T. Johnson, MSTM, MT(ASCP)SBB
*Editors*

In: Johnson ST, Puca KE, eds.
*Transfusion Medicine's Emerging Positions: Transfusion Safety*
*Officers and Patient Blood Management Coordinators*
Bethesda, MD: AABB Press, 2013

# 1

# *What's in a Title?*

## COLLEEN McGUINNESS SLAPAK, MS, MT(ASCP)SBB

BLOOD TRANSFUSIONS CAN SAVE LIVES. IN THE UNITED States (US), approximately 41,000 units of blood are transfused each day in emergency rooms, during surgical procedures, and for lifesaving cancer therapy.[1] Almost 21 million blood components were transfused in the US in 2011 and one in every 10 hospital admissions with a procedure will include a transfusion.[2,3]

However, blood transfusions are also associated with adverse events and other complications. Mounting evidence shows that the potential for adverse transfusion complications is significant, leading to unexpected therapeutic interventions that negatively affect the entire health-care system. In 2012, a consortium of physicians convened by The Joint Commission and the American Medical Association (AMA) identified blood transfusion as one of five specific treatments or procedures that needed urgent attention to reduce overuse and improve health-care quality for patient safety.[4]

Colleen McGuinness Slapak, MS, MT(ASCP)SBB, Transfusion Safety Director, Community Blood Center/Community Tissue Services, Dayton, Ohio
The author has disclosed no conflicts of interest.

This book explores two emerging positions in transfusion medicine: the managers of transfusion safety and patient blood management (PBM) programs. Using evidence-based best practices, the individuals in these new positions search for that balance between the lifesaving potential of blood transfusions and the use of safe alternatives whenever possible.

## Defining the Program

The exact number of transfusion safety, PBM, or similarly titled programs throughout the world is not known. Although the common objective of all these programs is patient safety, the descriptions, scope, terms, and definitions of these programs vary widely. Some possible definitions used in these programs are listed below.

**Transfusion Safety** is a broad term that includes one or more processes along the "vein-to-vein" continuum of care, from donor management and blood inventory management through patient transfusion management, blood utilization review, hemovigilance, and clinical outcome. Transfusion safety may also include clinical research on transfusion-related issues and emergency preparedness to ensure an adequate supply.

**Blood Conservation** is defined by some as the use of multiple strategies to reduce patients' exposure to allogeneic blood components.[5] These strategies include the use of surgical techniques and pharmaceutical products. Although bloodless surgical procedures are a large part of this program's strategy, the facility and patient determine to what extent they will consider the use of allogeneic blood.

**Blood Management** or patient blood management (a recent modification to clarify that the term is not about blood inventory) can be defined in several ways. AABB uses the wording "Patient blood management is an evidence-based multidisciplinary approach to optimizing the care of patients who might need transfusion."[6] This definition has also been adopted by the National Health Service (United Kingdom). The National Blood Authority (Australia) defines PBM as "the management and preservation of patients' own blood to reduce or avoid the need for blood transfusion."[7] The Society for the Advancement of Blood Management (SABM) uses the definition: "the timely application of evidence-based medical and surgical concepts designed to maintain hemoglobin concentration, optimize hemostasis, and minimize blood loss in an effort to improve patient outcome."[8]

## Program Models in 2012

A survey was conducted in 2012 to capture a snapshot of the current transfusion safety/PBM programs in existence.[9] This survey was completed by 108 respondents from known programs: 35 (32%) from the US; 67 (62%) from Canada; and 6 (6%) from other countries including the United Kingdom, India, Argentina, and Australia. Despite the small size of the survey and the fact that some respondents did not answer all questions, the results can provide useful information for the development of new programs.

As expected, the majority of programs identified by the survey are within a hospital or hospital group (74%). The remaining programs (26%) are facilitated through blood centers, provincial (Canada) offices, or university settings. Although most programs are directed by a physician, the survey focused on the program manager. These managers may be formally called officers, coordinators, supervisors, specialists, or leads. The professional background of survey respondents were as follows: 42% nursing (77% US, 24% Canada); 52% laboratory (9% US, 72% Canada); and 6% physicians or other job descriptions. Additional detail on the various program models is included in later chapters.

More than 30 different program manager titles were reported by survey respondents; the most common variations included the terms transfusion safety (50%), transfusion (18%), and blood management (16%) as part of the title. Other titles included the terms conservation (7%), quality (7%), and hemovigilance (4%). Specific titles were as diverse as blood utilization coordinator, technical lead transfusion medicine, medical laboratory specialist, clinical resource nurse for intravenous therapy, medical services coordinator, and others. From survey comments, it appears that program managers maintain their original title regardless of program modifications and expansion of goals.

Funding for programs differ as well. For instance, in Canada some programs are funded through the government. In the US, 64% of the programs are supported by hospital departments; of those, 57% received support from laboratory medicine, 19% from nursing, and 19% from a quality department.

Survey participants were asked to document activities included as part of their program. Common activities were divided into four categories: transfusion safety, PBM, documentation review, and research and development. Table 1-1 displays the responses received. Participants could select one or more functions performed in each category. Survey

## Table 1-1. Survey Results Listing Standard Program Activities

|  | Overall (%) | US (%) | Canada (%) |
|---|---|---|---|
| **PATIENT/TRANSFUSION SAFETY** | | | |
| Patient identification | 84 | 90 | 72 |
| Blood administration | 94 | 100 | 89 |
| Appropriate ordering practices | 87 | 94 | 81 |
| Transfusion reactions | 88 | 97 | 83 |
| Incidents and near-miss events | 84 | 84 | 78 |
| **PATIENT BLOOD MANAGEMENT** | | | |
| Limit blood loss through phlebotomy | 34 | 45 | 20 |
| Optimize patient hemoglobin levels before surgery | 48 | 45 | 41 |
| Minimize perioperative blood loss | 63 | 71 | 52 |
| Point-of-care monitoring during surgery | 37 | 52 | 20 |
| Blood utilization review | 91 | 97 | 85 |
| **DOCUMENTATION AND REVIEW** | | | |
| Transfusion guidelines development | 73 | 86 | 66 |
| Transfusion committee or peer review participation | 78 | 86 | 72 |
| Blood inventory management | 67 | 71 | 63 |
| Patient outcome review | 52 | 54 | 19 |
| **RESEARCH AND DEVELOPMENT** | | | |
| Massive transfusion protocol | 63 | 77 | 55 |
| Emergency preparedness/disaster planning | 31 | 29 | 33 |

results on additional activities such as transfusion-related education, development of specific protocols, and methods of data collection are not included here.

Most respondents indicated that their programs include commonly practiced patient transfusion safety activities (>80%). PBM activities show mixed results, although blood utilization review is included in most programs (91%). If one compares titles to activities, managers are just as likely to have "transfusion" in their title as "blood management" in both the US and Canada.

Almost 45% of survey respondents indicated they have been in their position for 5 years or less (US 74%, Canada 30%). However, the majority of programs (US 54%, Canada 95%) have been in existence for over 5 years. Forty-three percent (43%) of programs have been active for longer than 20 years (US 39%, Canada 44%). For programs developed within the last 5 years, over 60% of these managers have "transfusion safety" in their titles. All but one of the managers who documented his/her title as using the term "blood conservation" have been in the position for at least 6 years. Can it then be interpreted that titles are changing with the latest evidence-based literature and practices? As new evidence-based practices are implemented and the pressure to improve resources and reduce costs in health care continues, it will be interesting to follow the development of new programs and those who manage them.

## Hemovigilance

Hemovigilance can be defined as the monitoring and reporting of adverse events associated with blood collection and transfusion. The goal of hemovigilance is to improve transfusion safety and blood donor health. As noted in the above-mentioned survey, 88% of those respondents included monitoring of transfusion reactions as part of their duties. When asked whether transfusion reactions were being recognized and reported effectively at their institutions, only 15% of respondents responded positively. Only 35% indicated that they included audit mechanisms to detect adverse transfusion events that should have been reported. In the US, 17 of 35 respondents (49%) are either enrolled in the US National Healthcare Safety Network (NHSN), Biovigilance Component Module, or intended to enroll by the end of 2012. In Canada, 41 of the 67 respondents (61%) currently participate in the Transfusion Transmitted Injury Surveillance System (TTISS), which is a program within the Public Health Agency of Canada (PHAC) where hemovigilance data are reported.

## Training

There are only a few formal training programs for transfusion safety or blood management programs. Survey respondents identified that training for these roles is primarily through professional experience (65%), networking with others in a similar role (53%), and attending national meetings (40%) such as those of AABB and the Society for the Advancement of Blood Management (SABM). Other methods include use of an orientation program through a provincial government or professional society (Canada), an orientation program through a consulting group, direct training by a current role manager or predecessor, and self-education using available literature. Only 7% to 8% of respondents indicated use of a formal training program.

Commercial consultant groups have been actively involved in the development and implementation of programs. Thirteen respondents (14%) indicated that they used a consultant to advise, assist, or develop their program.

The majority of survey respondents (77%) agreed that a formal certification program should be developed in the future. However, many questioned whether such certification is currently practical and cost-effective because of the small number of professionals and the broad range of activities practiced.

## Moving Forward

The survey did not cover two significant areas of a well-designed transfusion safety or PBM program. A successful program should have an active multidisciplinary team that includes physicians, nurses, and clinical laboratory scientists (medical technologists). A member of the facility's senior management should also be included to ensure that the program objectives align with the facility's strategic goals and mission, and to provide authority for projects defined by the team. The inclusion of a pharmacist is recommended to provide expertise on the expanding use of pharmaceuticals as alternative solutions to treat anemia and reduce bleeding episodes. Representatives from the blood center should also be included to provide additional expertise in transfusion medicine and blood inventory management.

Information technology is also a significant area that a transfusion safety or PBM program should address. The majority of survey respondents (80%) are actively involved with data collection and review. Over 60% perform manual data collection methods to include chart review and audits. Over 60% also indicate that they use commercial spreadsheet tools. A growing number of programs use software developed specifically and marketed for transfusion safety and PBM programs.[9]

# Conclusion

Quality patient transfusion safety programs should continually evolve with development of effective, evidence-based methods. Methods should be based on accurate data collection and timely analysis of those data by the transfusion committee or assigned review body. Implementation of new methods (eg, clinical practice guidelines) need to be enforced and education provided to ensure success of the program. Only then can the program provide a safe, efficient, and measurable solution to ensure that the right patient receives the right treatment—blood or otherwise—in the right amount, at the right time, for the right reason.

# Acknowledgment

Thanks are due to the managers of transfusion safety and PBM programs for sharing their information through the survey discussed. Thanks also go to colleagues who contributed questions and helped edit the survey, including Kate Gagliardi, Melanie Jorgenson, Catherine Shipp, Nancy Dunbar, Kim Maynard, Joe Thomas, and Nanci Fredrich.

# References

1. Who needs blood? Bethesda, MD: AABB, 2013. [Available at http://www.aabb.org/resources/bct/pages/bloodfaq.aspx (accessed August 11, 2013).]
2. The 2001 Department of Health and Human Services. 2011 national blood collection and utilization survey report. Washington, DC: DHHS, 2013. [Available at http://www.aabb.org/programs/biovigilance/nbcus/Documents/11-nbcus-report.pdf (accessed August 11, 2013).]
3. Wier LM, Pfuntner A, Maeda J, et al. HCUP facts and figures: Statistics on hospital-based care in the United States, 2009. Rockville, MD: Agency for Healthcare Research and Quality, 2011. [Available at http://www.hcup-us.ahrq.gov/reports.jsp (accessed August 11, 2013).]
4. Proceedings from the national summit on overuse (July 8, 2013). Oakbrook Terrace, IL: The Joint Commission, 2013. [Available at http://www.jointcommission.org/overuse_summit/ (accessed September 23, 2013).]
5. Blood conservation versus bloodless surgery. [Available at http://www.mybloodsite.com/content/blood-conservation-programs-and-bloodless-surgery (accessed September 23, 2013).]
6. Patient blood management. Bethesda, MD: AABB, 2013. [Available at http://www.aabb.org/resources/bct/pbm/Pages/default.aspx (accessed August 11, 2013).]

7. Definition and rationale for PBM. Lyneham ACT, Australia: National Blood Authority, 2013. [Available at http://www.blood.gov.au/sites/default/files/documents/pbmsc-governance-arrangements_0.pdf (accessed August 11, 2013).]
8. What is patient blood management? Englewood, NJ: SABM, 2013. [Available at http://www.sabm.org (accessed August 11, 2013).]
9. McGuinness-Slapak C. Survey conducted and results presented at Nursing II: Patient Blood Management and Transfusion Safety Workshop. AABB Annual Meeting and CTTXPO, Boston, MA, October 7, 2012.

In: Johnson ST, Puca KE, eds.
*Transfusion Medicine's Emerging Positions: Transfusion Safety
Officers and Patient Blood Management Coordinators*
Bethesda, MD: AABB Press, 2013

# 2

# *Transfusion Safety in the 21st Century*

## JOSEPH THOMAS, RN, BSN

 PATIENT SAFETY HAS EMERGED IN THE 21ST CENTURY as a force to be reckoned with. Although interest in patient safety has never been greater, the concept is not a new concept. Initially spoken millennia ago, the directive "primum non nocere" (first do no harm) has become a central tenet for contemporary medicine. However, despite the good intentions of hospitals and health-care providers, in 1999 the Institute of Medicine released a report[1] estimating that 44,000 to 98,000 patients die annually as a result of medical error in hospitals. While transfusion-related errors and adverse events are only a small percentage of overall health-care-related complications, the following discussion will explore how the path to achieve optimal transfusion safety must mimic that of the patient safety journey over the past decade.

As with patient safety, transfusion safety is by no means novel. Dr. Bernard Fantus, known as the father of modern day blood banking, wrote this over 85 years ago: "As blood transfusion is a trying, even dangerous procedure to the recipient, the indications for it should be drawn

Joseph Thomas, RN, BSN, Senior Transfusion Safety Nurse Consultant, Strategic Healthcare Group LLC, Indianapolis, Indiana
The author has disclosed no conflicts of interest.

strictly and rather narrowly...throughout the injection the patient should be carefully observed for any unfavorable reaction. Failure to recognize these early symptoms may be responsible for a fatal result."[2] Almost a century later, these words should resonate powerfully among the readers of this book. Transfusion safety is being recognized by many organizations as a national patient safety initiative, and professionals within the scientific community who focus on improving transfusion safety are at the leading edge of this important initiative.

## The 21st Century: Blood Safety

The latter part of the 20th century was a troubling time in the era of blood safety. The emergence of human immunodeficiency virus and hepatitis as transmissible agents through the blood supply resulted in widespread concern by health-care providers and patients alike. During that period, thousands of patients acquired one of these life-threatening pathogens through blood transfusion and the public's perception of blood safety suffered for nearly 30 years as a result. For many years, the main concern of health-care providers and the public with blood transfusion related to "blood safety."[3] Blood safety focused primarily on the content within the bag of blood itself. Even today many health-care professionals and patients still consider disease transmission as their greatest concern related to transfusion.

However, blood safety has made remarkable improvements over the past two decades. This has been the result of multiple evolving technologies, safety procedures, and regulatory measures. The extensive system of safeguards in blood collection includes: donor education; donor screening, selection, and deferral procedures; postdonation blood product quarantining; highly sensitive assays to detect infectious disease; and donor tracking and notification when infectious disease is identified in a blood sample. Sustaining and continuously improving blood safety requires anticipating and responding to emerging pathogens and other threats. This requires an evolving system of technologies and processes used throughout the chain of blood collection, processing, storage, and transfusion. Blood providers, product vendors, academic researchers, health-care providers, and others continue to develop and implement new means for responding to higher demands for safety and emerging threats. Although technology and safety procedures vastly reduce the risks of contracting disease associated with blood transfusion, these protections are not perfect, and health risks from emerging transfusion-transmitted disease remain. As new pathogens and other threats to blood safety emerge, new means to counter these will be needed.

## Current Transfusion-Related Adverse Events

With the dramatic reduction in disease transmission through blood transfusion, other noninfectious risks have become the leading causes of mortality and morbidity related to transfusion. Although the rank and order of these adverse events have changed some over the past 5 years, the leading causes of transfusion-related mortality reported to the Food and Drug Administration (FDA) have consistently been: 1) transfusion-related acute lung injury (TRALI); 2) hemolytic transfusion reactions (non-ABO and ABO); 3) transfusion-associated circulatory overload (TACO); 4) bacterial/microbial infection; and 5) anaphylaxis (see Table 2-1).[4]

However, the actual number of transfusion-related deaths is likely underreported as suggested by recent studies and reports from active surveillance systems. This seems to be the case especially for hemolytic reactions,[5-7] TRALI,[8,9] and TACO.[10,11] The underreporting of transfusion-related adverse events, along with several strategies to address this safety gap, are discussed later in this chapter.

Although blood safety has improved dramatically over the years, new efforts to improve safety must be redirected to focus on the entire process—vein-to-vein transfusion safety.

## Vein-to-Vein Transfusion Safety

Transfusion safety addresses all aspects of the transfusion process from donation to transfusion (Fig 2-1). It is truly a vein-to-vein concept incorporating all of the products, technologies, and practices related to blood collection, processing, testing, ordering, and administration. Although most of the public's attention and national health-care dollars have been focused on the processing and testing of blood components, the ordering and administration of blood has received little attention. Over the years, hospitals and clinicians have left transfusion safety to blood providers and transfusion medicine specialists. Now that the risk profile of blood transfusion has changed, if blood safety is to continue improving, the responsibility for transfusion safety will have to expand to the hospital level among the clinicians involved with the actual ordering and transfusion of blood.[12] Transfusions are not a benign procedure, and

## Table 2-1. Transfusion-Related Fatalities[4]

| Complication | FY08 No. | FY08 % | FY09 No. | FY09 % | FY10 No. | FY10 % | FY11 No. | FY11 % | FY12 No. | FY12 % | Total No. | Total % |
|---|---|---|---|---|---|---|---|---|---|---|---|---|
| TRALI* | 16 | 35 | 13 | 30 | 18 | 45 | 10 | 33 | 17 | 45 | 74 | 37 |
| HTR (non-ABO) | 7 | 15 | 8 | 18 | 5 | 13 | 6 | 20 | 5 | 13 | 31 | 16 |
| HTR (ABO) | 10 | 22 | 4 | 9 | 2 | 5 | 3 | 10 | 3 | 8 | 22 | 11 |
| Microbial Infection | 1 | 15 | 5 | 11 | 2 | 5 | 4 | 13 | 3 | 8 | 21 | 11 |
| TACO | 3 | 1 | 12 | 21 | 8 | 20 | 4 | 13 | 8 | 21 | 35 | 18 |
| Anaphylaxis | 3 | 7 | 1 | 2 | 4 | 10 | 2 | 7 | 2 | 5 | 12 | 6 |
| Other | 0 | 0 | 1† | 2 | 1† | 3 | 1† | 3 | 0 | 0 | 3 | 1 |
| Totals | 46 | 100 | 44 | 100 | 40 | 100 | 30 | 100 | 38 | 100 | 198 | 100 |

*These numbers include both "TRALI" and "possible TRALI" cases.[10,11]
†Other: FY2009: Hypotensive Reaction[12]

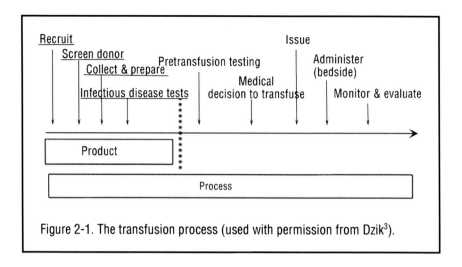

Figure 2-1. The transfusion process (used with permission from Dzik[3]).

complacency or lack of competence can result in poor patient outcomes. In fact, several of the most significant risks associated with blood transfusion reside with the transfusion process rather than the unit of blood. These adverse events often occur as a result of a failure in the transfusion process.

Although errors or adverse events may occur during any step in the transfusion process, the discussion that follows will focus on the areas with the most significant opportunities for improvement: medical decision to transfuse (including informed consent), blood administration, and patient monitoring and evaluation.

## Medical Decision to Transfuse

The ordering of blood component therapy involves a complex and important physician decision designed to weigh the benefits and risks of transfusion while also considering potential alternatives. Often overlooked when a clinician considers the concept of transfusion safety, the transfusion order is arguably the most important step in the transfusion safety chain. This is also the step most commonly ignored when evaluating the root-cause analysis of a transfusion error or near-miss. It is hard to argue with the fact that a transfusion error or adverse event cannot occur if the blood transfusion wasn't ordered in the first place. However, most physicians in the United States have never received formal training on blood component therapy in medical school or residency, so their transfusion training lacks standardization and is often more aligned with habits, misconceptions, and myths.

Wide variation in transfusion practice has been well-documented in nearly every medical and surgical specialty.[13,14] The variation in transfusion practice is known to exist among developed countries,[15] different hospitals, and even between physicians at the same hospital sharing the same specialty and patient populations.[16] In addition, transfusion audits by the blood bank or quality department frequently report high percentages of transfusions ordered outside of hospital-established criteria.[17,18] The documented rate of transfusion order noncompliance has been as high as 72%.[19] The wide variation in transfusion practice and noncompliance with evidence-based guidelines leads to unnecessary blood component exposure and avoidable patient harm.

## Informed Consent for Blood Transfusion

Consent for transfusion is a process—not simply the completion of a form—requiring a primary care provider (physician, nurse practitioner, or physician's assistant) to discuss the risks, benefits, and alternatives to transfusion with the patient, and/or the patient's family or guardian. Transfusion informed consent is a necessary element of the physician-patient relationship because transfusion is an invasive procedure (a tissue transplant) with definable significant risks. Meeting this ethical and regulatory obligation need not be complicated. Unfortunately, meaningful discussion between a physician and patient before transfusion that is comparable to a discussion before any other invasive procedure seldom occurs. One audit found that a signed informed consent document was absent in 9.2% (59/642) of medical records that included a transfusion episode.[20] Even when informed consent does occur, several studies report that patients remembered very little, if any, of the informed consent discussion.[21,22] Two very important questions emerge. Are patients truly being informed of the benefits, risks, and alternatives to blood component therapy? Are patients making informed choices about transfusion?

## Blood Administration/Patient Identification

Two of the leading causes of transfusion-related mortality, TACO and hemolytic reaction secondary to ABO incompatibility, are associated with blood component administration and the transfusionist's role. Data from the Serious Hazards of Transfusion (SHOT) report[23] in the United Kingdom indicate that transfusion of an incorrect blood component accounts for the largest proportion of all adverse events and is a frequent cause of mortality and morbidity associated with transfusion in the United States. Based on events recognized and reported to the New York State Health Department, Linden et al[5] calculated the risk of ABO mistransfusion was 1 in 12,000 units. Reports throughout other developed nations with mature hemovigilance programs report similar findings.[6,7] Therefore, safe and accurate blood administration is a critical component of the transfusion safety chain. This consists of verifying, *at the bedside,* that the right patient is getting the right blood product.

## The Right Patient

Several trends that should cause concern have been reported in case studies and published audits related to inadequate practices surrounding patient identification before blood administration.[24] Anecdotally, it has been reported that some nursing units perform the dual identification process at the nurse's station or outside of the patient's room rather than at the bedside. In one multicenter audit, verification of patient identification before transfusion was not conducted (two signatures on the transfusion record as required) in 7.7% of the transfusion episodes reviewed.[20] These noncompliant records often had only one signature or in some case no signatures at all. Failing to verify patient identification at the bedside and with two qualified individuals compromises patient safety and puts the patient at risk for a transfusion error.

## The Right Product

One of the more common deficiencies identified during routine audits of blood administration is the failure to verify the physician order before transfusion. Failure to complete this simple step may lead to transfusion of the wrong blood component (eg, plasma instead of platelets) or improperly preparing the correct blood component (nonirradiated instead of irradiated). Either of these errors can lead to disastrous consequences, including transfusion-associated graft-vs-host disease (GVHD).

## The Infusion Rate

Ordering the lowest effective dose for transfusion therapy and selecting the appropriate infusion rate for each blood component is essential to minimize the potential for patient harm. Ordering excessive blood components or administering blood more rapidly than tolerated can overwhelm the recipient's circulatory system and lead to TACO. The reported incidence of TACO has escalated over the past decade—which is likely multifactorial in nature and a combination of better reporting and recognition, and also because of an aging and increasingly comorbid patient population. The rate of TACO caused by all blood components ranges from approximately 1% to 8%.[25,26] The 2012 FDA transfusion-related mortality report indicated TACO was among the most commonly reported causes of death, accounting for nearly 20% of reported deaths over the past 5 years.[4] Several factors have been noted to contribute to the increasing incidence of TACO.

- Lack of recognition by clinicians of TACO as a leading cause of transfusion-related morbidity and mortality.[27,28]
- Lack of attention to fluid balance, particularly in elderly patients and those with predisposing comorbidities (eg, cardiac and renal impairment, hypoalbuminemia, and fluid overload).
- The culture among clinicians to routinely order 2 units of Red Blood Cells (RBCs) without consideration of ordering a single RBC unit followed by a reassessment.
- The absence of a *physician-ordered* infusion rate for each blood component as part of the transfusion order. If an infusion rate is not indicated, nursing staff will often determine the rate, which may vary by nurse and department.
- Lack of evidence-based guidelines for the infusion rate of non-RBC components. Most published guidelines and hospital policies recommend that non-RBC components be infused "as quickly as tolerated."[29] This often translates to "as fast as possible," ranging from 10 to 30 minutes. Although this rate is appropriate in patients who are actively bleeding, many patients now receive non-RBC components as a prophylactic measure (before surgery). In these patients this infusion rate can lead to TACO.

With transfusion error and TACO remaining two of the leading causes of transfusion-related mortality, more ownership and accountability for transfusion safety must shift onto the clinical teams and the transfusionist.

**Monitoring and Evaluation**

The early recognition and management of transfusion reactions is critical; delays can significantly affect patient outcomes. In many cases, the amount of blood infused is directly related to the severity of the transfusion reaction. Hospital transfusion services have long been suspicious that transfusion-related adverse events are underrecognized and underreported by their clinical colleagues at the bedside. Published studies have reported the incidence of transfusion reactions to be approximately

1% to 4%,[23,31,32] depending upon the patient population being transfused. However, the rate of adverse transfusion reactions reported to US
hospital transfusion services was 0.24% in the 2011 National Blood Collection and Utilization Survey Report.[30] The gap between these figures is
significant, with an order of magnitude separating the two reported
findings.

Several recent audits have highlighted the underrecognition and underreporting of transfusion-related adverse events.[31,32] One multicenter
review[32] evaluated 5739 transfusion episodes and identified 136 adverse
events (2.4%). Only 71 of the 136 (52%) were recognized as transfusion-
related and reported to a physician. Only 30 of the 136 (22%) were properly reported to the transfusion service. Within the study, the most common adverse events that went unreported to the physician and the transfusion service were febrile and pulmonary reactions (see Table 2-2).

Based upon these and other published reports there appear to be two
major contributing factors to the low reporting of transfusion reactions—both underrecognition AND underreporting. The concept that
transfusion reactions are underrecognized is supported in studies that
report suboptimal patient monitoring practices during transfusion (eg,
vital signs, observation). Not only do policies for vital sign requirements
during blood administration often vary by hospital and region, noncompliance with such requirements is well-documented in the literature.
Some reports state that vital signs were not documented according to
hospital policy in 18% to 33% of the cases reviewed.[20,24] Failure to monitor vital signs and observe the patient at regular intervals throughout
the transfusion can lead not only to delays in reaction recognition but
also in failure to recognize the reaction altogether.

In order to gain a better understanding of the issue, some focused
questions must be asked: What are the underlying issues contributing to

| Table 2-2. Poor Reporting of Transfusion Reactions[32] | | |
| --- | --- | --- |
| Total transfusions = 5739 <br> Adverse events = 136 | **Yes** | **No** |
| Reported to a physician | 71/136 (52%) | 65/136 (48%) |
| Reported to the transfusion service | 30/136 (22%) | 106/136 (78%) |

clinical knowledge and performance gaps in transfusion management? What hospital strategies can be implemented to close the gaps related to transfusion safety? Lastly, what global strategies can be implemented to optimize transfusion safety?

## Understanding Transfusion Safety Gaps

The etiology of these safety gaps is multifactorial and multidisciplinary in nature. Understanding the genesis of clinical knowledge and performance gaps in transfusion safety is also critical to develop before implementing process improvement strategies.

### Education and Training Deficiencies

Lack of formal training in medical schools and residency programs in evidence-based transfusion guidelines has been recognized as one contributing factor behind the transfusion safety gaps. For physicians, knowledge is usually passed down from senior residents and attending physicians, both of whom may have inaccurate or antiquated knowledge. Nursing school curricula have also been known to provide little to no skill-based training in blood transfusion safety. Many hospitals attempt to provide nursing education on blood administration and transfusion reactions; however, much of this education is provided via self-learning packets or computer-based training, which are marginally effective at best. Considering that blood transfusion is the most commonly employed medical procedure in hospitals, it seems that correction of these deficiencies in education and training should be a priority.

### Complacency

Although blood transfusion is not a completely benign therapy, the majority of blood components are ordered and administered without incident. One risk of performing a procedure such as blood transfusion on a routine basis is the tendency to become complacent and fail to follow all policy requirements or recognize the onset of a serious adverse event. High-volume blood transfusion departments are especially susceptible to this risk. Root-cause analysis following cases of severe or fatal transfusion reactions have reported the role of complacency during the patient identification process or in the failure to recognize the adverse event and stop/discontinue the transfusion in an appropriate manner.[33]

## Limited Coordination, Communication, and Teamwork

It's no mystery that the world of laboratory professionals is very different from that of clinicians and nurses. This stems from differences in training, professional responsibilities, regulatory oversight, work environment, and often even personality. In addition, both groups typically have limited professional interaction, which is not conducive to developing an environment of communication and teamwork. This can lead to challenges when facing potentially tense clinical situations (eg, transfusion reactions, massive bleeding, etc).

## Lack of Transfusion Safety "Ownership" by the Clinical Team

For the past three decades, transfusion safety has been something mainly left to the blood provider and the transfusion service. An expectation was set for the blood community by clinicians and patients alike to dramatically reduce or eliminate infectious disease from the blood supply. Although blood providers have reduced the risk of disease transmission through transfusion by 99.9%, the major causes of transfusion-related morbidity and mortality are noninfectious, serious hazards of transfusion. Several of these are directly related to clinical practice. However, while hospital transfusion services have remained the most regulated department in health-care facilities, clinical governing bodies and hospital accrediting organizations have been slow to establish requirements for clinicians. Several voluntary standards and requirements do exist [eg, those of AABB, College of American Pathologists (CAP)] but are not often well known by clinicians and nurses.

# Hospital Strategies to Improve Transfusion Safety

A multidisciplinary, multimodal strategy is required to improve the management of blood components and optimize transfusion safety. A comprehensive review of current hospital strategies to improve transfusion safety is beyond the scope of this chapter; however, several recommendations are outlined below.

## Formal Education/Skill-Based Training

It may take years for medical school and nursing school curricula to adopt standardized, formal training in patient blood management and transfusion safety. However, hospitals can help close these gaps by providing both regular education and training programs for their clinical staff. There is no one simple way to accomplish widespread physician education, so a multimodal strategy should be employed. Several academic residency programs require that their resident physicians yearly attend a live lecture or take an online program in evidence-based transfusion therapy as part of their training. Other hospitals arrange for periodic Continuing Medical Education (CME)-accredited programs by either in-house subject matter experts or visiting professors. If well-advertised by the hospital leadership and medical staff leadership, these events can be well attended. Department meetings, the hospital intranet, physician newsletters, and use of transfusion order sets or computerized physician order entry (CPOE) systems with practice guidelines have also been shown to be effective strategies for awareness and education.

Nurses are required to have periodic education in blood administration and transfusion reactions. This is most commonly provided as self-learning packets or as computer-based training programs. Although these are efficient tools to disseminate information to hundreds or thousands of nurses, they are known to be marginally effective. The use of simulation or skill-based training is an effective, yet rarely utilized, strategy because of increased allocation of hospital resources (mannequins, nursing/physician time). Expanding the use of skill-based training is a strategy that should be explored by education teams to close knowledge and performance gaps in transfusion safety. This can also be accomplished by incorporating teachable moments during regular blood administration audits on the nursing units.

Physicians and nurses want to provide the safest, most evidence-based care possible; many are just largely unaware of the current evidence as it relates to transfusion safety. Hospitals must take affirmative steps to provide, or even require, clinical education in patient blood management and transfusion safety.

## Blood Utilization Committees and Blood Utilization Oversight

As hospitals focus on becoming high-performing organizations, there is an increased need for oversight and monitoring to ensure that procedural safety measures are being practiced consistently. All hospitals are required to provide blood utilization oversight; however, the manner in which they do so is not clearly defined. While many hospitals wisely choose to have a formal Blood Utilization Committee (BUC), having a committee alone will not ensure transfusion safety. An effective BUC should be multidisciplinary with representatives from the high-blood-use departments. It should be an active committee with a focus on quality. Some key responsibilities should include establishing guidelines for the appropriate use of blood components, monitoring blood utilization and transfusion practice in an effective manner, exploring proactive strategies to reduce the need for transfusion in high-risk patients, and providing a continuous feedback loop to clinical departments and individual physicians on transfusion performance. The BUC is the nucleus of a comprehensive patient blood management program and a critical element to hospital transfusion safety.

A meaningful way to perform utilization oversight for transfusion practice is important. There is also a need for accountability when transfusion safety measures are not followed, regardless of the individuals involved. The BUC must be given "teeth" via the Medical Executive Committee and the hospital by-laws. If regular noncompliance with the hospital transfusion guidelines is identified, the BUC should be given the authority to address this in a peer-to-peer fashion with the backing of hospital leadership.

## Technologies

Hospitals are investing billions of dollars into electronic health-care systems with the intent of improving patient safety and reducing the risk of medical error. Although these systems are far from perfect, they can be customized or designed to improve transfusion safety. Computerized physician order entry is quickly becoming a standard of care in US hospitals and can be part of a comprehensive strategy to improve physician ordering practices.[34] Evidence-based transfusion guidelines can be built within a CPOE design, including a requirement that the physician designate the appropriate indication before ordering a transfusion. Physicians may choose the "other" indications, but they should still be required to enter a clinical indication. Some of these systems can also be utilized to create reports with department- and provider-specific ordering trends that can be very useful for BUC review.

Multiple technologies have also been designed to reduce the risk of harm associated with blood administration. Hospital identification bands placed on patients at sample collection, blood transport bags with combination locks, "smart" refrigerators for blood dispensing, barcoding technologies, and even radio-frequency identification have all been used by hospitals to supplement the patient identification process and reduce the risk of human error. For blood administration, "smart" infusion pumps are being employed to minimize risk of circulatory overload.

Unfortunately, because of the absence of financial incentives and the high cost associated with some of these resources, many hospitals have not yet implemented these technologies.

## Transfusion Safety Officers

Hospitals are establishing champions in many areas of patient safety such as wound care, fall prevention, and medical safety. Why not for transfusion safety? Several European countries and Canada have established Transfusion Safety Officers (TSOs) in their larger institutions; however, this role is relatively new in the United States. As noted earlier, transfusion safety outside the laboratory has been the responsibility of the blood bank even though no one in the transfusion service routinely orders or administers blood components. This gap in clinical ownership and accountability can contribute to serious lapses, misunderstandings, knowledge gaps, and errors. The principal role of the hospital TSO is to fill this gap and take ownership of patient blood management and transfusion safety outside of the laboratory.

## National and Global Strategies to Improve Transfusion Safety

National and global strategies to improve transfusion safety are being considered worldwide. Some strategies are mandated, while implementation of others is voluntary but strongly urged.

### Mandated Performance Measures

Required performance measures focused on patient blood management and transfusion safety could reiterate the commitment of professional societies to patient safety. They could give hospitals clear direction and a strong incentive to monitor key performance indicators as they relate to transfusion ordering practices and blood administration. More important, national performance measures would empower professionals dedicated to transfusion safety to advocate for improvement within their facilities. At a minimum, such measures should focus on: transfusion ordering practices (compliance with hospital guidelines, transfusion dosing); blood administration (patient identification, patient monitoring); and management of transfusion reactions (recognition and reporting). These metrics could be tracked collaboratively by the transfusion service and quality department and be part of the BUC dashboard. Hospitals committed to quality, organizations involved in the accreditation of hospitals, and regulatory bodies concerned with patient safety would all be served by national performance measures related to transfusion safety.

## Biovigilance

The United States National Healthcare Safety Network (NHSN) Biovigilance component strongly advocates a coordinated approach to the collection and analysis of data on transfusion-related adverse events.[35] Similar systems in other developed countries appear to have improved transfusion safety.[36,37] Improvements will require some changes to the culture of US hospitals, because the environment for years has been one of medicolegal liability, and the failure to disclose errors and near-miss events. The success of the biovigilance network depends upon the ability of the clinical staff to accurately identify and properly report near-misses and transfusion-related adverse events. A similar approach in other fields (aviation and nuclear safety) has contributed to marked improvements in safety of those areas.

## Patient Blood Management Programs

Patient blood management (PBM) can be defined as an evidence-based, multidisciplinary approach to optimizing the care of patients who might need transfusion.[38] Interest in PBM has never been greater for US hospitals, many of which are looking to develop comprehensive programs. Although multiple factors are driving this international interest, patient safety is at the forefront. Many professional organizations and regulatory agencies, including AABB,[39] The Joint Commission,[40] Society for the Advancement of Blood Management,[41] and the federal Department of Health and Human Services, actively support the growing efforts in PBM by providing resources, guidelines, and performance measures. PBM programs have reported significant success in reducing unnecessary blood transfusions while improving patient outcomes.

# Conclusion

Blood transfusions will continue to save lives when used in a safe and evidence-based manner. However, blood transfusion is a transplant of living tissue and can result in avoidable harm when used inappropriately. This has been well known by transfusion medicine specialists but has not been well disseminated into the general medical and nursing communities. Blood component safety will remain an important focus, but the more comprehensive concept of vein-to-vein transfusion safety should be the focus of health care today. If transfusion safety is to continue to improve, this change will have to take place at the hospital level among the clinicians (caregivers or health-care professionals) involved with the actual ordering and transfusion of blood.

# References

1. Kohn LT, Corrigan JM, Donalson MS, eds. To err is human: Building a safer health system. Washington, DC: National Academy Press, 1999.
2. Fantus B. The therapy of the Cook County Hospital. Therapeutics 1937;109:128-31.
3. Dzik WH. Emily Cooley Lecture 2002: Transfusion safety in the hospital. Transfusion 2003;43:1190-9.
4. Fatalities reported to FDA following blood collection and transfusion—annual summary for fiscal year 2012. Rockville, MD: CBER Office of Community Outreach and Development, 2012. [Available at http://www.fda.gov/BiologicsBlood Vaccines/SafetyAvailability/ReportaProblem/TransfusionDonationFatalities/ UCM346639.htm (accessed August 26, 2013).]
5. Linden JV, Paul B, Dressler KP. A report of 104 transfusion errors in New York State. Transfusion 1992;32:601-6.
6. Robillard P, Itaj NK, Corriveau P. ABO incompatible transfusions, acute and delayed hemolytic transfusion reactions in the Quebec hemovigilance system— Year 2000 (abstract). Transfusion 2002;42(Suppl):25S.
7. Andreu G, Morel P, Forestier F, et al. Hemovigilance network in France: Organization and analysis of immediate transfusion incident reports from 1994 to 1998. Transfusion 2002;42:1356-64.
8. Kopko PM, Marshall CS, MacKenzie MR, et al. Transfusion-related acute lung injury: Report of a clinical look-back investigation. JAMA 2002;287:1968-71.
9. Rana R, Fernandez-Perez ER, Khan SA, et al. Transfusion-related acute lung injury and pulmonary edema in critically ill patients: A retrospective study. Transfusion 2006;46:1478-83.
10. Popovsky MA. Transfusion-associated circulatory overload: The plot thickens (editorial). Transfusion 2009;49:2-4.
11. Murphy EL, Kwaan N, Looney MR, et al. Risk factors and outcomes in transfusion-associated circulatory overload. Am J Med 2013;126:357.e29-38.
12. Brooks JP. Reengineering transfusion and cellular therapy processes hospitalwide: Ensuring the safe utilization of blood products. Transfusion 2005;45(Suppl):159S-171S.
13. Frank SM, Savage WJ, Rothschild JA, et al. Variability in blood and blood component utilization as assessed by an anesthesia information management system. Anesthesiology 2012;117:99-106.
14. Snyder-Ramos SA, Möhnle P, Weng YS, et al for the Investigators of the Multicenter Study of Perioperative Ischemia; MCSPI Research Group. The ongoing vari-

ability in blood transfusion practices in cardiac surgery. Transfusion 2008;48: 1284-99.

15. Cobain TJ, Vamvakas EC, Wells A, et al. A survey of the demographics of blood use. Transfus Med 2007;17:1-15.

16. Bennett-Guerrero E, Zhao Y, O'Brien SM, et al. Variation in use of blood transfusion in coronary artery bypass graft surgery. JAMA 2010;304:1568-75.

17. Corwin HL. Transfusion practice in the critically ill: Can we do better? Crit Care Med 2005;33:232-3.

18. Friedman MT, Ebrahim A. Adequacy of physician documentation of red blood cell transfusion and correlation with assessment of transfusion appropriateness. Arch Pathol Lab Med 2006;130:474-9.

19. Rothschild JM, McGurk S, Honour M, et al. Assessment of education and computerized decision support interventions for improving transfusion practice. Transfusion 2007;47:228-39.

20. Thomas J, Parks J, Hannon T. Nursing performance and knowledge gaps in blood management and transfusion safety (abstract). Transfusion 2009;49(Suppl):243-4A.

21. Chan T. Consenting to blood: What do patients remember? Transfus Med 2005;15:461-6.

22. Adams K, Weiss K, Tallch D. Blood transfusion: The patient's experience. Am J Nurs 2011;111(9):24-30.

23. Annual SHOT Report 2012 Summary. Manchester, UK: SHOT, 2012. [Available http://www.shotuk.org/wp-content/uploads/shot-summary-2012.pdf (accessed August 5, 2013).]

24. Novis DA, Miller KA, Howanitz PJ, et al. Audit of transfusion procedures in 660 hospitals: A College of American Pathologists Q-Probes study of patient identification and vital sign monitoring frequencies in 16,494 transfusions. Arch Pathol Lab Med 2003;127:541-8.

25. Bierbaum BE, Callaghan JJ, Galante JO, et al. An analysis of blood management in patients having a total hip or knee arthroplasty. J Bone Joint Surg Am 1999;81:2-10.

26. Li G, Rachmale S, Kojicic M,et al. Incidence and transfusion risk factors for transfusion-associated circulatory overload among medical intensive care unit patients. Transfusion 2011;51:338-43.

27. Narick C, Triulzi D, Yazer M. Transfusion-associated circulatory overload after plasma transfusion. Transfusion 2012;52:160-5.

28. Thomas J, Baffa A, Nienhaus S, Hannon T. Underrecognition and underreporting of the pulmonary complications of transfusion (abstract). Transfusion 2012;52 (Suppl):235A.

29. Sink BL. Administration of blood components. In: Roback JD, Grossman BJ, Harris T, Hillyer CD, eds. Technical manual. 17th ed. Bethesda, MD: AABB, 2011:617-29.

30. Department of Health and Human Services. The 2011 national blood collection and utilization survey report. Washington, DC: DHHS, 2013.

31. Narvios AB, Lichtiger B, Newman JL. Underreporting of minor transfusion reactions in cancer patients. MedGenMed 2004;19;6:17.

32. Thomas J, Parks J, Hannon T. Mismanagement of transfusion-related adverse events (abstract). Transfusion 2010;50(Suppl):50A.

33. Gafou A, Georgopoulos G, Bellia M. Review in the literature of the new solutions to an old problem: Human error in transfusion practice. Haema 2005;8:598-611.
34. Rothschild JM, McGurk S, Honour M. Assessment of education and computerized decision support interventions for improving transfusion practice. Transfusion 2007;47:228-39.
35. Centers for Disease Control and Prevention. The National Healthcare Safety Network (NHSN) Manual: Biovigilance component. Atlanta, GA: CDC, 2010.
36. Stainsby D, Jones H, Asher D, et al. Serious hazards of transfusion: A decade of hemovigilance in the UK. Transfus Med Rev 2006;20:237-82.
37. Chapman CE, Stainsby D, Jones H, et al. Ten years of hemovigilance reports of transfusion-related acute lung injury in the United Kingdom and the impact of preferential use of male donor plasma. Transfusion 2009;49:440-52.
38. AABB. Patient blood management. Bethesda, MD: AABB, 2013 [Available at http://www.aabb.org/resources/bct/pbm/pages/default.aspx (accessed August 5, 2013).]
39. Becker J, Shaz B for the Clinical Transfusion Medicine Committee and the Transfusion Medicine Section Coordinating Committee. Guidelines for patient blood management and blood utilization. Bethesda, MD: AABB, 2011.
40. The Joint Commission. Patient blood management performance measures project. Oakbrook Terrace, IL: The Joint Commission, 2011. [Available at http://www.jointcommission.org/patient_blood_management_performance_ measures_project (accessed July 29, 2012).]
41. SABM resource center. Englewood, NJ: Society for the Advancement of Blood Management, 2013. [Available at http://www.sabm.org/learning-resources (accessed August 5, 2013).]

In: Johnson ST, Puca KE, eds.
*Transfusion Medicine's Emerging Positions: Transfusion Safety
Officers and Patient Blood Management Coordinators*
Bethesda, MD: AABB Press, 2013

# 3

# *The Evolution of Two New Positions*

JEFFREY WAGNER, BSN, RN, AND
NANCI FREDRICH, RN, BSN, MM

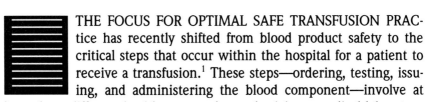 THE FOCUS FOR OPTIMAL SAFE TRANSFUSION PRAC-
tice has recently shifted from blood product safety to the
critical steps that occur within the hospital for a patient to
receive a transfusion.[1] These steps—ordering, testing, issuing, and administering the blood component—involve at
least three different health-care workers, physicians, medical laboratory
scientists (technologists), and nurses with no single department solely
responsible for the entire process. Central to patient safety within this
process is the appropriateness of the transfusion. In addition, with an
ever-increasing number of studies suggesting an association of adverse
patient outcomes with blood transfusion, avoidance of transfusion is becoming a more desired therapy. With this movement in transfusion therapy, two new positions have emerged—transfusion safety officers (TSOs)
and patient blood management coordinators (PBMCs). The growth in
the number of health-care professionals who hold these positions is a

Jeffrey Wagner, BSN, RN, Seattle, Washington, and Nanci Fredrich, RN, BSN, MM,
Transfusion Safety and Blood Management Officer, BloodCenter of Wisconsin, Milwaukee, Wisconsin

direct reflection of the changes occurring in transfusion medicine. This chapter provides a brief overview of the history of these positions and describes the driving factors behind the changes—still taking place today—that influence the development of TSO and PBMC positions.

## Brief History of Blood Transfusion

The history of blood transfusion spans hundreds of years with most discoveries having been made since the early 1900s. Attempts at blood transfusion were made as early as the mid-1600s, when transfusion of blood from animals to human beings was first documented. As that type of transfusion was not successful, the conclusion was made that blood is not universal between species. Early transfusions of blood from humans to other humans resulted in many deaths, and for a time, transfusion was outlawed. As knowledge about physiology and anatomy was gained, interest in transfusion was renewed in the late 19th century. Because there was no knowledge about blood storage, transfusions were administered directly from the donor to the patient.[2-4] Again, transfusions were associated with a high mortality rate.

The discovery of the ABO blood types by Dr. Karl Landsteiner at the dawn of the 20th century aided the ability to provide compatible blood transfusions. Scientists also discovered how to use sodium citrate to prevent coagulation and how to use refrigeration to extend the shelf life of the product. The Fantus Clinic in Chicago, known as the first "blood bank" in the United States, was established in 1937.[2] As is often the case, war and armed conflicts advanced the technology for manufacturing of blood components and the knowledge to manage excessive bleeding. During World War II both albumin and liquid plasma were introduced and used as first-line resuscitative fluids. Physicians who were accustomed to using stored blood in the battlefield also wanted blood available back home for their hospitalized patients. This led to a rapid growth of independent blood banks in hospitals and communities. In the 1960s another milestone advanced the production and availability of blood components and expansion of blood banks. The introduction of plastic containers for the collection and storage of blood made it possible to separate whole blood into its components within a closed system and revolutionized the concept of component therapy—transfusing only the specific component that the patient needs.[5,6] Yet, even as blood transfusion and the manufacturing of blood components advanced, so did the knowledge of its adverse effects and the need to manage patients without it.[2-4]

In the 1960s in the United States the quality of the donor pool was questioned when it was discovered that 50% of donors were paid for their blood donation and thus may have had an incentive to be less than truthful during screening. In addition, although donations were tested for syphilis, it was noted that many people developed jaundice after receiving a transfusion. There was no coordinated system for managing donors or blood component processing and thus potentially infected donors could not be tracked and deferred from future donations. In the 1970s the Department of Health, Education, and Welfare proposed a National Blood Policy in an attempt to unify and promote standardized practices. With the concern that the incidence of hepatitis was three times more likely in paid donors than volunteer donors, the Food and Drug Administration began requiring that blood products be labeled with the origin of the donor (paid or volunteer). Further developments in the testing and screening of donors improved the safety of the blood components, but the emergence of unknown diseases and how to test for them remained an issue.[2,3,7]

The transmission of hepatitis through blood transfusion and the AIDS epidemic in the 1980s heightened concerns with the safety of donated blood and the problems of testing for these transfusion-associated infectious diseases. The human immunodeficiency virus (HIV) was identified in the early 1980s but a test to detect HIV antibodies was not developed until 1985. Although serologic testing for HIV and hepatitis B and C viruses dramatically reduced the incidence of transmission of these diseases by blood transfusion, the demand for safer blood and bloodless medicine increased. The medical community began to re-evaluate blood transfusion practice and ask critical questions. Are blood transfusions necessary? Are we harming our patients?[5,7-9]

By the end of the 20th century, great strides had been made for prevention of transfusion-transmitted disease. Major contributors included increased scrutiny of blood donors and an extensive health history questionnaire, introduction of nucleic acid testing (NAT) for HIV and hepatitis, improved sensitivity of EIA testing for viral markers, prestorage leukocyte reduction, and application of good manufacturing practice for blood component preparation. The risk for acquiring HIV or hepatitis C by transfusion was around 1 in 2 million. In the early 2000s bacteria detection in platelet products also decreased the risk of transfusion-transmitted bacterial infection.[8] With this marked reduction in the risk of transfusion-transmitted infectious diseases, the focus shifted to noninfectious complications, including those related to inappropriate use and human error.

## Brief History of Bloodless Medicine

Bloodless medicine and alternatives to blood transfusion were driven by several factors. The origin of "bloodless medicine" is largely attributed to Jehovah's Witnesses for their stance on refusal of blood transfusion in their care. Their painstaking efforts to find physicians and hospitals that would provide medical care and perform surgeries without blood transfusions were, without a doubt, fundamental to the development of bloodless medicine and surgery programs.[7]

One of the early pioneers and surgeons to take on the challenge of performing bloodless surgery was Dr. Denton Cooley. First performed in the 1970s, open-heart surgery with the use of the heart-lung machine required that a patient be crossmatched for 25 units of blood.[7] In 1977, Cooley published his experience in performing successful open-heart surgery without blood transfusion.[10] The news quickly spread and soon programs appeared in California, Michigan, Ohio, New Jersey, and also in European countries. These programs contributed greatly to the knowledge base of bloodless medicine and surgery. The approaches and strategies developed and refined by these physicians to maximize hematopoiesis and minimize blood loss have been instrumental for the growth of PBM programs today.[11] The emerging awareness of the risks of transfusion (both infectious and noninfectious) and the desire of patients to avoid blood transfusion based on personal or medical (rather than religious) reasons also contributed to the proliferation of bloodless medicine programs.

The collective experience from these bloodless medicine programs has supported the shift for lower transfusion thresholds, treating patients based on symptoms rather a number, and use of appropriate alternative treatments to support all patients who may need a transfusion.[12] Many centers expanded the bloodless medicine concept to include "patient blood management," a patient-centric, multidisciplinary approach serving *all* patients, regardless of their preference or acceptance of a blood transfusion, with the goal of improving patient outcome by integrating all available techniques to reduce or eliminate allogeneic blood transfusions.[7,11] What began as an advocacy has now become a motivating force for best practice in transfusion medicine.

## Bloodless Medicine/Blood Management Program Coordinator

Historically, many bloodless medicine coordinators or PBMCs were Jehovah's Witnesses, as their beliefs supported those of patients who refused transfusion. As bloodless medicine moved to incorporate blood conservation techniques for all patients, program coordinators came from more diverse backgrounds.[7]

The key to a successful bloodless medicine or PBM program is a coordinated team approach to patient care supported throughout the institution.[13] The most crucial role is that of the PBMC, who integrates the program within the organization and becomes the key contact for patients, families, and physicians. The PBMC works closely with a program medical director who is the liaison to the various medical specialties in the institution. Success is dependent on everyone in the institution understanding and supporting the desires of the patient during their hospital course. The PBMC ensures that for those patients who do not accept allogeneic blood, the patient's wishes are honored and respected. The coordinator is the person who has an initial discussion with the patient when a desire for bloodless surgery or treatment is expressed. He or she is also responsible for determining what options for treatment are acceptable to the patient and to communicate the desires and options to the physicians and medical team. An explanation of various techniques or equipment used in surgical procedures is part of the education for all patients and families. The treatment plan for the patient must be communicated throughout the institution. The PBMC must ensure that pertinent health-care records such as advance directive, refusal of blood components, and documentation of conversations with the patient and acceptable options identified during the discussion are completed and become part of the patient medical record. The coordinator may also see patients weeks in advance of elective procedures to optimize red cell production and identify any existing anemia and treat its causes.[7,11,13]

## Development of the TSO Position in the United States

Job descriptions of TSO-like positions in the United States date back several decades. Since the 1960s, this position has had multiple titles including blood bank nurse coordinator, transfusion service liaison, and transfusion nurse specialist to name a few. These pioneer positions were held by nurses who were not considered part of the nursing department, but instead functioned under the direction of a hospital blood bank director or the medical director of a transfusion service. The job duties of these early TSOs ranged from monitoring blood bank refrigerators scattered throughout a hospital to collecting blood from donors and even performing compatibility testing. Included in their job description were activities such as educating staff nurses about blood administration, teaching residents compatibility testing, and investigating transfusion reactions. They organized hospital transfusion committee meetings and analyzed blood usage for the institution.

## Other Drivers for this New Role

As described in Chapter 2, transfusion safety involves much more than blood product safety. Although infectious risks of transfusion have declined, risks of an error occurring along the continuum of patient care still exist. The three high-risk areas for error include patient sample collection, medical decision to transfuse, and bedside administration of the blood product, all of which occur *outside* the laboratory.[1] The complex processes for a transfusion are multidisciplinary and no department has sole responsibility, least of all the laboratory. Thus, any successful change or improvement in patient safety regarding transfusion is limited unless there is an individual with responsibility for the transfusion care outside the laboratory.

Besides reducing the risk of transfusion errors, other drivers for the recent movement to establish TSO positions are the limited training in transfusion medicine for physicians, loss of transfusion review committees at many hospitals, and the growth and merger of health-care systems. Education on the risks and indications for the use of blood in medical schools is minimal. A recent survey of postgraduate (year 1) residents at a single center in the United States showed that 41.4% of the residents had received no lecture in transfusion medicine and 34.5% received only a single lecture.[14] With limited formal training it is no wonder that physicians learn transfusion principles from their mentors and colleagues, and develop misconceptions and practices that are not evidence-based. A hospital can benefit from a dedicated TSO who can provide physicians and nursing staff with continuing education and guidance on the appropriateness of, and indications for, blood transfusion, component administration, and transfusion safety.

Although the Joint Commission has required ongoing review of physician's transfusion practice since 1961, this review varies among hospitals. Over the years it seems that the emphasis for having a transfusion review committee has been reduced.[15] In some facilities, the committee either meets infrequently or no longer exists because of poor attendance, lack of physician input, and lack of authority to make changes. In addition, reviews of transfusion practice are often retrospective, even up to 3 months after the transfusion event. For some hospitals this review is conducted under the purview of the hospital quality management department and thus can be easily lost amid other quality initiatives, especially ones associated with reimbursement. An individual to facilitate and collect, analyze, and report meaningful physician ordering practices can help revive a transfusion review committee.[16] As hospitals have grown and become more specialized or merged with other institutions, "silos" in thinking and behavior can arise. It often then becomes more challenging to maintain adequate communication and integration between departments within the facility. Poor or mis-communication between hospital staff can be one cause for errors.[16] As explained in subsequent chapters, nurses and medical laboratory scientists often do not speak the same "language." An individual to bridge this "communication divide" and foster understanding between the two departments will inevitably improve the transfusion process.

## Increasing Recognition

As the awareness of the TSO position spread, hospitals and blood centers became interested in the role of the TSO and how it could benefit patients and enhance the work of health-care teams. In the United States, early adopters to create TSO and TSO-like roles included University of Washington Medical Center, University Hospitals of Cleveland, Dartmouth-Hitchcock Medical Center, and Virginia Mason Medical Center, among others. Physicians in transfusion medicine began to see the value of such a position and possibilities for the future.

AABB sparked continued interest by promoting nursing at its annual meetings and creating a nursing special interest group. At its 2001 Annual Meeting, AABB offered specific education programs as a means of reaching clinicians outside the laboratory. Program topics included bloodless medicine in the pediatric setting, and the work of the Ontario Transfusion Coordinators. Gradually the focus has swung to the role and job functions of TSOs. At about the same time, nurses and TSOs became active in numerous AABB committee activities involving projects in transfusion safety or PBM. One of the first references to "transfusion safety officer" in the literature appeared in a 2003 article "Patient Safety and Blood Transfusion: New Solutions" published in *Transfusion Medicine Reviews.*[16] The authors stated that "A new position, the transfusion safety officer (TSO), has been developed in some nations to specifically identify, resolve, and monitor organizational weakness leading to unsafe transfusion practice." In the preceding year, Dr. Walter Dzik presented the TSO position as one of the "human solutions" to improving transfusion safety in the hospital at his Emily Cooley Memorial Lecture at the 2002 AABB Annual Meeting.[1] By 2006, a description of the qualifications, selection, work, and a business case proposal for a TSO appeared in print.[17] Additional publications highlighted the work TSOs were performing at hospitals and blood centers throughout the United States, Canada, Australia, and Europe.[18-20]

## The Numbers Grow

By October 2008 there were approximately 14 TSO positions identified in the United States, including six positions in Seattle, two in Ohio, and one each in Georgia, New Hampshire, New Jersey, Texas, Virginia, and Wisconsin. In contrast, 201 US hospitals responding to the 2011 National Blood Collection and Utilization Survey reported having a TSO, with over 60% of these positions being full-time.[21] Following cues from TSOs in Canada and Europe, the role of the US-based TSO now is filled by medical laboratory scientists and physician assistants as well as nurses. The role of the TSO has expanded beyond the walls of the transfusion service with the ultimate goal of improving patient safety within the spectrum of transfusion practice (discussed in other chapters).

## Looking into the Future

In recent years, transfusion medicine and bloodless medicine have both evolved toward a focus on the concept of patient blood management—appropriate use of blood components and multiple strategies to reduce or eliminate allogeneic transfusions with emphasis on improved outcomes for all patients (Fig 3-1). Both TSOs and PBMCs play a critical role in the promotion of transfusion safety and the development of PBM programs. Individuals in these positions have focused their efforts beyond the walls of the transfusion service laboratory, resulting in an integrated approach for appropriate and safe transfusions. They have promoted evidence-based, best practice treatment for all patients including those who choose to exclude transfusion as part of their care. TSOs and PBMCs

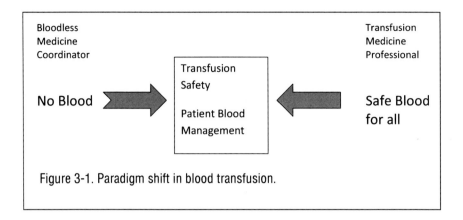

Figure 3-1. Paradigm shift in blood transfusion.

help colleagues understand and respect the wishes of the patient and then create a treatment plan that manages anemia, optimizes hemostasis, reduces blood loss, and provides appropriate blood transfusions to improve patient outcomes. As more and more organizations recognize the benefits of PBM programs, it is likely that TSO and PBMC positions will increase in number and perhaps even in the scope of their responsibilities.

# References

1. Dzik WH. Emily Cooley Lecture 2002: Transfusion safety in the hospital. Transfusion 2003;43:1190-99.
2. Network for the Advancement of Transfusion Alternatives. History and development of transfusion medicine. Malakoff, France: NATA, 2000. [Available at http://www.nataonline.com/np/31/history-and-development-transfusion-medicine (accessed August 28, 2013).]
3. Highlights of transfusion medicine history. Bethesda, MD: AABB, 2010. [Available at http://www.aabb.org/resources/bct/Pages/highlights.aspx (accessed August 28, 2013).]
4. Red gold: The epic story of blood. Blood history timeline. New York: WNET, 2002. [Available at http://www.pbs.org/wnet/redgold (accessed August 28, 2013).]
5. Blajchman MA. Transfusion medicine – the coming of age of a new specialty. Transfus Med Rev 1987;1(1):1-3.
6. Greenwalt TJ. A short history of transfusion medicine. Transfusion 1997;37:550-63.
7. Seeber P. History and organization of blood management. In: Seeber P, Shander A, eds. Basics of blood management. 1st ed. Boston, MA: Blackwell Publishing, 2007:1-8.

8. Perkins HA, Busch MP. Transfusion-associated infections: 50 years of relentless challenges and remarkable progress. Transfusion 2010;50:2080-99.
9. Langone J. Fear of aids is only one reason some doctors are calling for bloodless surgery. TIME 1997;150(19):74-6.
10. Ott DA, Cooley DA. Cardiovascular surgery in Jehovah's witnesses: Report of 542 operations without blood transfusion. JAMA 1977;238:1256-8.
11. Shander A, Javidroozi M, Perelman S, et al. From bloodless surgery to patient blood management. Mt Sinai J Med 2012;79:56-65.
12. Farmer S, Webb D. Your body, your choice. Singapore: Media Masters, 2000.
13. Martyn V, Framer SL, Wren MN, et al. The theory and practice of bloodless medicine. Transfus Apheresis Sci 2002;27:29-43.
14. O'Brien KL, Champeaux AL, Sundell ZE, et al. Transfusion medicine knowledge in postgraduate year 1 residents. Transfusion 2010;50:1649-53.
15. Saxena S, Shulman IA. Resurgence of the blood utilization committee. Transfusion 2003;43:998-1006.
16. Dzik WH, Corwin H, Goodnough LT, et al. Patient safety and blood transfusion: New solutions. Transfus Med Rev 2003;17:169-80.
17. Wagner JD, AuBuchon JP, Saxena S, Shulman IA. Guidelines for the quality assessment of transfusion. Bethesda, MD: AABB, 2006.
18. Williams L. The TSO's role in hemovigilance and patient blood management. AABB News 2011;13(7):6-8.
19. Eckert K, Lima A, Urbanek A. How transfusion safety officers improve patient care in Canada. AABB News 2008;10(2):29-31.
20. Bielby L, Stevenson L, Wood E. The role of the transfusion nurse in the hospital and blood centre. ISBT Science Series 2011;6:270-6.
21. Department of Health and Human Services. The 2011 National Blood Collection and Utilization Survey. Washington, DC: DHHS, 2013.

In: Johnson ST, Puca KE, eds.
*Transfusion Medicine's Emerging Positions: Transfusion Safety
Officers and Patient Blood Management Coordinators*
Bethesda, MD: AABB Press, 2013

# 4

# *Review of Roles: Transfusion Safety Officer and Patient Blood Management Coordinator*

## KIMBERLY J. MAYNARD, BSN, RN, OCN

 AS NOTED IN THE PREFACE, PATIENT BLOOD MANAGE-
ment (PBM) programs are still in their infancy, and no con-
sensus exists with regard to definitions, policies, processes,
or procedures. It is the same with the general roles and specific responsibilities of those who manage PBM activities.
This chapter offers one possible approach to the characterization of two
positions—the transfusion safety officer (TSO) and the patient blood
management coordinator (PBMC).

## Transfusion Safety Officer

The role of the TSO is to extend the transfusion service's quality assurance system to the clinical arena and standardize transfusion practices

Kimberly J. Maynard, BSN, RN, OCN, Nurse Coordinator, Dartmouth-Hitchcock Medical
Center, Lebanon, New Hampshire
The author has disclosed no conflicts of interest.

for the hospital or institution. In 2003, Dzik et al described the functions of hospital TSOs as promoting safe and effective transfusion therapy. These functions may include: 1) following the transfusion process by auditing the sample collection, blood request/delivery, and bedside administration; 2) tracking key indicators and errors/accidents; and 3) reporting to the transfusion committee.[1]

The TSO's role revolves around the ability to effect change at the bedside in order to provide optimal care to the patient during the transfusion episode. Chief responsibilities include functioning as an expert practitioner, educator, researcher, and consultant/change agent.[1] As an expert practitioner, the TSO is the critical link between the transfusion service and the bedside nurse to ensure that the transfusion process meets regulatory requirements and standards. This may include ensuring a rigorous patient identification check using two independent identifiers prior to initiating a transfusion, which is required for compliance with AABB *Standards for Blood Banks and Transfusion Services*.[2] A two-person check meets the requirements of The Joint Commission's National Patient Safety Goal to improve the accuracy of patient identification when administering blood components and collecting blood specimens.[3]

The TSO serves as a clinical resource to transfusionists, nurse educators, residents, phlebotomists, and laboratory technicians, and as a centralized contact for transfusion-related questions. He or she may coordinate or lead quality-improvement projects related to blood component use and blood administration. The goal is to continuously improve the transfusion process while providing a resource contact and compliance officer at the clinical end in order to provide the safest possible transfusion experience for the patient.[4]

**Educational Programs**

Development, implementation, and oversight of transfusion-related education programs are an essential part of the TSO's practice. Ongoing education of transfusionists and phlebotomists in appropriate patient identification during transfusion and at sample collection is instrumental to providing safe care. Providing in-service lectures on safe transfusion practice to nurses, residents, and blood bank staff is a frequent responsibility of the TSO. Projects may include implementation of, and education around, process improvement work and quality initiatives, such as the use of barcode technology or radio-frequency identification related to specimen collection and blood component administration. TSOs should remain current with the transfusion literature, standards, and guidelines related to blood component usage, transfusion techniques, and alternatives to transfusion as they are often called upon to provide recommendations to hospital transfusion committees, transfusion services, and clinicians. Their recommendations should be developed on the basis of clinical findings as well as an understanding of the literature and regulatory requirements. Maintaining a current resource library of educational materials for transfusion best practices and alternatives to transfusion is suggested in order to have the most recent best practice information readily available.

## Policies and Procedures

TSO responsibilities typically include establishing, monitoring, and maintaining safety protocols to comply with hospital policies and regulatory requirements. This is achieved by creating or updating policies and procedures for the administration of blood components, alternatives to transfusion, and quality assurance of the institution's blood utilization program. Writing and/or reviewing transfusion policies and procedures can help to ensure the TSO understands the bedside transfusion process and can identify potential problems related to compliance and workflow constraints. One of the TSO's goals should be to ensure appropriate and safe bedside transfusion practices that reflect current evidence-based practice. A second goal should be involvement in blood utilization review in order to contribute to improving patient safety and outcomes, as well as compliance with standards and regulations.

## Blood Product Orders

The TSO needs to understand and then develop, or assist in developing, local criteria for blood component requests and orders based upon current transfusion guidelines and evidence from the literature. The TSO assists by providing information on appropriate transfusion ordering and administration practices to those involved in developing the institution's transfusion criteria and to the teams that create order/order entry and documentation pathways. This is particularly important as hospitals transition from paper-based blood orders, ordering practices, and documentation to electronically driven transfusion decision support aids and mechanisms to document transfusion administration. Just-in-time provider order entry education may be accomplished via written information on transfusion order forms or computerized physician (provider) order entry (CPOE), using institutionally approved indications and transfusion thresholds. Recommendations to control active bleeding and treat causes of anemia may be included. Because it is imperative that CPOE reflects the current transfusion practice and requirements of the institution, the TSO is involved along with the transfusion service medical director and other staff in creating the institution's criteria.

## Transfusion Reactions and Incidents

Timely reporting of incidents, errors, and near-misses related to transfusion, as well as transfusion reactions, is a responsibility of transfusionists or clinicians involved in the care of the patient. These events should be reported during or shortly after any transfusion event. The TSO provides education to those involved in transfusion, which allows them to recognize and report reactions and incidents via the proper mechanism. Investigation and follow-up of transfusion reactions can be performed by the TSO in collaboration with the transfusion service medical director. The TSO collects transfusion reaction data and monitors the following for completion: transfusion reaction investigations, interpretation notes written by medical staff, and stated patient outcomes.

Investigation and follow-up of transfusion-related incidents, errors, and near-misses are often performed by the TSO, in lieu of someone in the quality department. Oversight of these investigations is needed to provide feedback to those involved, as well as those affected, to ensure that corrective action takes place. Data and outcomes are tracked and final disposition reported to the hospital quality department or transfusion committee.

## Communication

The TSO serves as a liaison between the transfusion service and nursing staff, which contributes to better communication and collaboration between these departments and to improved patient outcomes.[5] The TSO provides periodic updates to the Transfusion/Blood Utilization Committee, the blood bank, leadership councils, and quality-related committees on issues related to blood utilization and transfusion safety. As a liaison between the transfusion laboratory and clinicians, the TSO is an important representative to the transfusion committee and reports on an ad hoc or regular basis each time the committee meets. Specific reports may include updates on key transfusion processes or indicators (eg, blood administration and documentation, blood wastage), specific improvement projects, and blood utilization [eg, number/percentage of Red Blood Cell (RBC) units transfused by department, service line, or provider]. The TSO should also report on transfusion issues related to compliance and activities to facilitate improvement within the transfusion process. The TSO may help to coordinate the committee's agenda in collaboration with the chair.

## Practice Audits

The TSO audits transfusion practices to ensure compliance with local transfusion policies and procedures as well as state and federal regulatory requirements. Audits may consist of a vein-to-vein review from patient sample collection to final transfused blood component or may encompass specific portions of the process. Audits to be considered include: how often informed consent for transfusion is obtained, transfusion is completely documented, or blood orders meet established criteria; the number of blood requests compared to transfused components; blood delivery; and bedside administration. It is the responsibility of the TSO, in conjunction with the transfusion service medical director, to determine the type and number of audits to be conducted on a yearly basis. Bedside transfusion audits may be conducted based on a percentage of the total transfusions administered or on an absolute number (such as 10 or 20) each month. Audit findings and summaries are presented to the medical director for signature and filing. Findings that indicate corrective action is required should be followed by the TSO until resolution and reported to the transfusion committee.

## Look-Backs

A TSO can be instrumental in coordinating look-back and recall procedures to identify at-risk recipients of blood and blood components from donors found to later have positive human immunodeficiency virus, hepatitis B virus, hepatitis C virus, and human T-cell lymphotropic virus antibody test results. Following the specific requirements and time frames as stipulated by the Food and Drug Administration (FDA) and Centers for Medicare and Medicaid Services (CMS), the TSO can organize the appropriate information for the transfusion service medical director's attention.

## Research

The TSO may design research projects or participate in transfusion-related research, such as clinical trials comparing methods of transfusion practice, as well as preparation of publications or presentations for scientific or clinical conferences. Depending upon the needs of the department to which the TSO reports, this may be part of the job expectation or it may fall to other individuals within the department.

## TSOs and Patient Blood Management

Although the TSO's specific job description, responsibilities, and reporting structure will vary from institution to institution, the overarching concept of the TSO role is to maintain patient safety throughout the transfusion process. Recently the transfusion community has focused attention on best clinical practice vs best transfusion practice. Adhering to more restrictive transfusion guidelines and practice, as advocated by several leading associations and societies, may decrease mortality resulting from transfusion. However, removing infectious, immunologic, and other risks of transfusion requires the optimization of clinical practice afforded by patient blood management (PBM).[6] TSOs may be called upon to function as practitioners of both transfusion safety and PBM. Depending upon the organization, the TSO may also be responsible for developing and/or coordinating part of the local or regional PBM program. See Appendix on CD-ROM for examples of job descriptions.

### Patient Blood Management Programs

There has been a surge in interest in the development of PBM programs as institutions begin to think about blood safety encompassing transfusion as well as alternatives to transfusion. The evolving concept of blood management includes "…the appropriate provision and use of blood components, and strategies to reduce or avoid the need for a blood transfusion, with the ultimate goal of improving patient outcomes and reducing costs."[7] A PBM program incorporates management of anemia, optimization of coagulation, blood conservation (limiting blood loss through phlebotomy, surgical techniques), autotransfusion techniques (eg, intra- and postoperative blood recovery, acute normovolemic hemodilution), and use of intraoperative hemostatic agents to minimize blood transfusion. In addition, the use of transfusion decision thresholds (conservative transfusion strategies, administration of single RBC units) is employed.[8]

Ideally, the local Transfusion/Blood Utilization Committee will help to drive implementation of a PBM program and offer support for initiatives. In order to provide education and guidance regarding decision thresholds for appropriate blood transfusion and alternative transfusion approaches, the TSO, in partnership with physician colleagues, can participate in hospital or unit-based rounds at locations that transfuse the most blood.[9] Opportunities for improvement are shared with participating groups as well as the local Transfusion/Blood Utilization Committee. Audits to be performed and data to be tracked include how often hospital-defined ordering criteria are met and whether appropriate transfusion alternatives are used.

## Patient Blood Management Coordinators

The roles of the PBMC and TSO in blood component safety, transfusion administration safety, and PBM may overlap or comprise two separate and distinct sets of responsibilities. Although these "separate" roles may be different in approach, they may not be altogether different in philosophy. Some hospitals have created job descriptions that combine the role of PBMC and TSO in order to pair the activities of PBM with transfusion safety. This person can thus promote appropriate blood utilization and conservation of blood resources along with alternatives to transfusion while also working to improve the transfusion-related quality process.

PBM, as an evidence-based medical and surgical approach, can bring together multidisciplinary practitioners to improve clinical outcomes and patient safety. Working cooperatively with other groups (eg, surgeons, administrators, transfusion medicine specialists) the PBMC assists in establishing programs such as a preoperative anemia management clinic to include anemia screening, diagnosis, and treatment, while employing established algorithms for preoperative blood work and testing. Optimizing patients' hemoglobin before surgery can decrease the use of perioperative RBC transfusions and associated complications.[10] Limiting blood losses through phlebotomy by consolidation of laboratory test orders, using the smallest possible blood collection volumes, and point-of-care testing is another example of PBM program development where the PBMC can offer assistance and expertise.

Because PBM programs track appropriate blood utilization, a focus of the PBMC is to lead and conduct blood utilization data collection and analysis to determine areas for focused improvement, including utilization audits and process improvements to decrease blood component waste. The PBMC may collaborate or interface with anesthesia providers to provide support for the process of acute normovolemic hemodilution during surgery.

Coordinating all aspects of the intraoperative blood recovery and reinfusion program (collection, washing, and reinfusion of concentrated red cells obtained from blood loss at the surgical field) can be a PBMC role, reporting to the medical director of the program. This includes oversight of policies and procedures related to intra- and postoperative recovery and reinfusion of red cells, monitoring of periodic quality assurance specimen collection and tests results to ensure that predefined criteria are met, and tracking evidence of initial and ongoing training by personnel who operate blood recovery equipment and reinfuse red cells.

Responsibilities specific to blood management may include:

- Develop goals for the PBM program.
- Counsel patients on alternatives to transfusion.
- Serve as liaison between "bloodless" patients and physicians/staff.
- Monitor revenue production and cost savings.
- Identify, implement, and evaluate blood conservation strategies.
- Monitor and report program performance.

# Overlapping Activities

### Creating a PBM Program

A PBMC or TSO is well-positioned to assemble and lead a working team to address aspects of PBM, drawing upon physicians, nurse leaders, quality managers, administrators, and patient groups. A step-wise, incremental approach to forming a PBM program may be required because of time and financial constraints. PBMCs/TSOs can spearhead or assist in collecting, organizing, and tracking data, as well as identify metrics to monitor and evaluate the effectiveness of the PBM program. Blood utilization data by department, service line, and provider can be tracked and compared internally or, if resources exist, against benchmarked metrics in the institutional group. It may be difficult to find comparison data nationwide in the US at the time of this writing. Collaboration with similar-sized transfusion services and PBM programs from other institutions may afford benchmarking data for comparison.

Although PBMCs/TSOs have a vested interest in promoting PBM and transfusion safety, they may not have the knowledge or expertise to develop this role. If local guidance from the transfusion service or surgical colleagues is not available, the PBMC/TSO should contact members of another organization that has already established such a program and seek their assistance. Established programs at other institutions may be willing to host a visit or offer resources and guidance telephonically. There are also organizations that offer tutelage in PBM and program implementation assistance for a fee.

## Hemovigilance

Hemovigilance activities may be undertaken by both TSOs and PBMCs. Local data capture of transfusion-associated adverse events with subsequent reporting to private or national systems may provide benefit to the reporting institution. These systems are designed to tabulate and analyze entered data and offer benchmark comparison to the institution. The United States Centers for Disease Control and Prevention (CDC) National Healthcare Safety Network (NHSN) Hemovigilance Module is one example. The NHSN seeks to improve patient safety and minimize unnecessary costs associated with transfusion-related adverse events. Participating hospitals may receive de-identified benchmarking data with comparison to similar-sized hospitals from AABB. AABB will analyze the group's hemovigilance data with the goal of developing interventions that will improve patient safety.

## Patient Engagement

Ideas to engage the patient in shared decision-making should be foremost in the mind of the TSO and PBMC, because patients actively involved in their health care achieve better outcomes and have lower health-care costs than those who are not actively engaged. Crucial elements for patient engagement include system support, providing patients with decision aids, collaboration, and teamwork.[11] Informing patients of the choices available to them is the next logical step in the process. Efforts to create and disseminate decision aids (which could include treatment benefits provided by an anemia clinic preoperatively, use of intraoperative blood recovery, and the risks/benefits of blood transfusion) is a project the PBMC/TSO could undertake with a team effort. Patient education might include the role for patients in their own care, as well as providing the appropriate decision aid(s) related to PBM. If the PBMC/TSO requires assistance to reach as many patients as possible, the help of hospital quality champions may be sought in order to provide patients with decision aids and to answer their questions.

# Conclusion

The PBMC's primary focus is on improving patient outcomes while reducing the use of allogeneic blood products, and the TSO's focus is usually on patient safety in transfusion. Regardless of their roles, they should be able to effectively interact, communicate, and work collaboratively with a variety of groups, including clinicians and nonclinical staff at all levels, and to demonstrate a strong ability to solve problems. As they consult with appropriate clinical services across multiple departments related to transfusion, blood component use, and alternative treatments, they need the experience and knowledge to articulate well-thought-out concepts, lead project teams, and serve as coach and teacher. Although TSOs and PBMCs may have different roles depending upon the institution and job description, they need to be versed and grounded in transfusion medicine practices and quality improvement processes in order to help provide the best possible outcomes for patients who receive transfusions or alternative treatments to transfusion.

# References

1. Dzik WH, Corwin H, Goodnough LT, et al. Patient safety and blood transfusion: New solutions. Transfus Med Rev 2003;17:169-80.
2. Carson TH, ed. Standards for blood banks and transfusion services. 28th ed. Bethesda, MD: AABB, 2012:32.
3. National patient safety goal (NPSG 01.01.01). Oakbrook Terrace, IL: The Joint Commission, 2013. [Available at http://www.jointcommission.org/assets/1/18/NPSG_Chapter_Jan2013_HAP.pdf (accessed August 12, 2013).]
4. Wagner J, AuBuchon JP, Saxena S, Shulman IA, et al for the Clinical Transfusion Medicine Committee. Guidelines for the quality assessment of transfusion. Bethesda, MD: AABB, 2006.
5. Slapak C, Fredrich N, Wagner J. Transfusion safety: Is this the business of blood centers? Transfusion JBSM 2011;51:2767-71.
6. Spahn D, Vamvakas E. Is best transfusion practice alone best clinical practice? Blood Transfus 2013;11:172-4.
7. Shander A, Javidroozi M, Perelman S, et al. From bloodless surgery to patient blood management. Mt Sinai J Med 2012;79:56-65.
8. Shander A, Javidroozi M. Strategies to reduce the use of blood products: A US perspective. Curr Opin Anesthesiol 2012;25:50-8.
9. Alexander L. A look at five elements involved in a PBM program. AABB News 2012;14(5):6-12.
10. Goodnough L, Shander A. Patient blood management. Anesthesiology 2012;116:1367-76.
11. Molyneux J. Patient activation: Real paradigm shift or updated jargon? Off the Charts. AJN blog for February 7, 2013. [Available at http://ajnoffthecharts.com/2013/02/07/patient-activation-real-paradigm-shift-or-updated-jargon// (accessed September 23, 2013).]

In: Johnson ST, Puca KE, eds.
*Transfusion Medicine's Emerging Positions: Transfusion Safety
Officers and Patient Blood Management Coordinators*
Bethesda, MD: AABB Press, 2013

# 5

# Models for Transfusion Safety Officers and Patient Blood Management Coordinators

NANCI FREDRICH, RN, BSN, MM, AND
JULIE DeLISLE, RN, MSN

 AN ORGANIZATION CONSIDERING THE BENEFITS OF A transfusion safety officer/patient blood management coordinator (TSO/PBMC) position has several options to consider. First, should an individual be hired to work within the organization or should the facility contract with another group for service?

Second, if hiring, what will the TSO/PBMC role be and where in the organizational hierarchy does the position belong? The newly created patient blood management (PBM) program requires forethought and planning and should be aligned with the organization's strategic goals and culture to be effective. An assessment of the models and the

Nanci Fredrich, RN, BSN, MM, Transfusion Safety and Blood Management Officer, BloodCenter of Wisconsin, and Julie DeLisle, RN, MSN, Transfusion Safety and Blood Management Officer, BloodCenter of Wisconsin, Milwaukee, Wisconsin

The authors have disclosed no conflicts of interest.

risk/benefit of each is a key factor for any institution in deciding how the position will fit into their organization.

Models to consider include a TSO/PBMC as a hospital employee, a contracted employee from the local blood supplier or other organizations who will be based in the institution, or a TSO/PBMC employed by the local blood supplier available on an as-needed basis to the local institution. Other unique partnerships between hospitals and blood centers or other organizations may develop by utilizing creative ideas that will result in an improvement of transfusion safety and blood management. Slapak et al conducted an informal survey in 2012 to determine demographic information about TSO/PBMC positions in the United States and Canada. Currently, the majority of TSOs are employed by hospitals (74%) while another 14% are employed by a blood center/supplier.[1]

## Hospital-Based Model

A hospital-based TSO functions very similarly to other hospital compliance or safety officers such as an infection control practitioner. The safety officer or hospital compliance position is focused solely on a key area of patient care that crosses all departments and services. A TSO focuses on all aspects of the blood transfusion spectrum within the hospital—from arrival of the blood components in the transfusion service to the completion of the transfusion, including monitoring for effectiveness of the transfusion and adverse events. Over time, functional "silos" can develop between departments within an organization or even between institutions within a health-care system.[2] These barriers cause communication failures and conflict, which can affect productivity. Creating an understanding of work performed in each department through cross-functional communication can be a role of the TSO. The TSO can be the liaison to various departments within a hospital to build collaborative relationships and enhance communication, thus changing transfusion practice and improving patient care.

### Reporting Structure

In looking at a hospital-based model for a TSO, one needs to determine where the individual will be housed (cost center), and to whom the TSO will report, both directly and indirectly. Another factor to consider is the scope and authority given to the TSO to implement change and to affect the transfusion process and practice. Within a hospital, a variety of departments could house the cost center and supervise the TSO and/or PBMC. These could include the transfusion service/blood bank, hospital quality improvement, nursing, or even the chief medical officer.

Basing the position in the transfusion service/laboratory will keep the position focused on blood components and all associated aspects within the spectrum of transfusion, from ordering to administration and post-transfusion monitoring. In this reporting structure, the TSO will become very aware of the regulations the transfusion service must meet as part of its accreditation process. This information can be shared with the nursing or the operating room staff to provide background for compliance. A TSO could report directly to the transfusion service medical director or transfusion service director/manager (see Fig 5-1). The TSO could be at a disadvantage in this instance, if the laboratory is a contracted service for the hospital. The TSO will need to learn to cross boundaries between two businesses that may have conflicting visions and needs. If based in the transfusion service, a TSO will need to establish contacts and develop relationships in hospital departments such as nursing, hospital quality, pharmacy, and the operating room.

On the other hand, placing a TSO/PBMC under the direction of the hospital quality improvement director, who often reports to the chief nursing officer, or vice president of nursing could be advantageous (see Fig 5-2). Quality improvement departments are often viewed as enforcers of accreditation requirements and as change agents for nursing and physician practice. Quality improvement departments frequently work

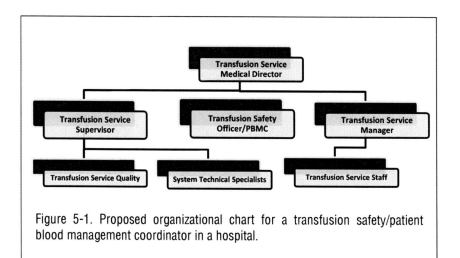

Figure 5-1. Proposed organizational chart for a transfusion safety/patient blood management coordinator in a hospital.

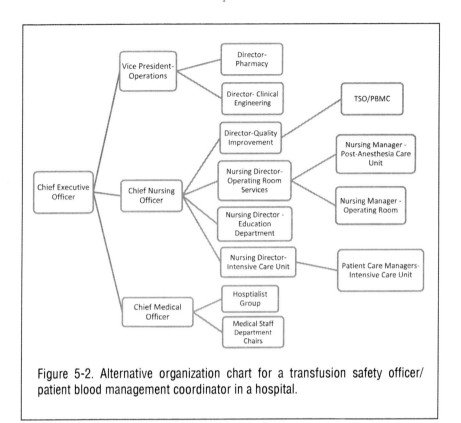

Figure 5-2. Alternative organization chart for a transfusion safety officer/ patient blood management coordinator in a hospital.

cross-functionally with areas other than nursing to create a quality environment throughout the institution. Staff in quality management departments often demonstrate project management skills that could be useful to a TSO/PBMC. As accreditation organizations such as AABB or The Joint Commission increase their focus on transfusion safety, and standards for PBM are developed, hospitals and quality improvement departments will increasingly look to TSOs to assist in this area. The potential growth of PBM programs will also create the need for these positions in an institution or health-care system. A disadvantage of basing a TSO in a quality improvement department is the risk this person may be tasked with other job responsibilities not relating directly to transfusion safety, thus diluting the purpose of the position.

Of the TSOs employed by hospitals or health-care systems, 66% report to the laboratory or transfusion medicine department, 20% are based in a nursing department cost center, and 11% report to a quality assurance/improvement department.[1] In 2005, Brooks[3] proposed that a

TSO be the sole person to have control over all transfusion-related activities within a hospital. He even proposed the TSO have the title of vice president of transfusion affairs (VPTA), report directly to the chief executive officer, and interact with any and all departments and services where transfusion activities occur. The VPTA would have the authority to make immediate decisions in any situation with a potential safety issue in regards to transfusion. An example described was a potential safety problem with a blood storage refrigerator outside the blood bank. The VPTA would have the authority to immediately take the refrigerator out of service and not allow it to be used again until authorized. The VPTA would not have to request permission from anyone in the department where the refrigerator is stored or from the medical director of the transfusion service. If deemed necessary, a process-improvement plan would immediately be put into place to correct the problem, the protocol for use would be rewritten if needed, and staff would be educated on the new policy before allowing the blood storage refrigerator to be placed back into service. In a similar model in the nursing department, the TSO could report directly to the chief nursing officer with the same type of authority described by Brooks.

## How Does a TSO Improve Blood Transfusion within a Hospital?

Building relationships outside the transfusion service or nursing department is the key to changing transfusion practice. The new TSO starts by asking to be a guest at as many meetings as possible. Such meetings would include those of the nursing governance or practice council, quality or quality improvement council, nursing unit staff meetings, pharmacy staff meetings, and even clinical engineering staff meetings. Attendance at medical staff meetings or department meetings provides an opportunity to make introductions and explain a TSO's role so physicians can put a name and face together. Not everyone knows what a TSO is and what the job entails. The TSO gets actively involved in the blood utilization committee or, if such a committee doesn't exist, he or she should discover where blood usage data are reported and become a member of that group. The TSO needs to learn what committees are discussing blood usage but may not be part of the larger blood utilization committee. It is important to ask questions, such as: What are the hospital's blood utilization guidelines? How are data on blood usage gathered and shared among clinicians? How are blood transfusions ordered? What is the nursing policy for blood administration? Answers to these inquiries can lead to projects and areas of improvement for the TSO to address.

Examples of projects and process improvements for the TSO/PBMC were gathered as part of Slapak's survey[1] in 2012. TSO/PBMCs were involved in one or more of the following projects at their institution (hospital or blood center):

- Patient identification.
- Blood administration nursing policy.
- Appropriate ordering practices.
- Transfusion reaction recognition and reporting.
- Incidents and "near-miss" events related to transfusion.
- Limiting blood loss through phlebotomy.
- Optimizing patient hemoglobin levels (anemia clinics).
- Minimize perioperative blood loss.
- Point-of-care testing during surgery.
- Blood utilization review (data collection and reporting) and patient outcome reviews.
- Participation in hospital transfusion committees including transfusion guidelines.
- Hospital blood inventory projects.

TSOs and PBMCs will become heavily involved in education of health-care providers and patients as a result of some of these projects. Physicians and nurses traditionally receive minimal education about blood component preparation, indications for transfusion, or alternatives to transfusion. As more research/studies are conducted on the risks and benefits of transfusion and evidence-based practices are established, the TSO can educate and promote transfusion practice based on evidence rather than tradition. Patients and their families trust that nurses and other health-care workers provide them with the information to make informed decisions surrounding blood transfusion.[4] Through a collaborative effort, TSO/PBMCs can optimize transfusion practice and improve patient outcomes. Projects can include education about transfusion and blood administration that meets accreditation requirements and standards, alternatives to transfusion, and regular presentation of blood usage data to both physicians and nurses.

Blood usage data sharing creates an awareness of actual physician transfusion ordering practice and highlights the variation in practice within the institution. Ongoing data about physician transfusion practice promotes best practice in transfusion and can result in decreasing blood transfusions in an institution. The establishment of evidence-based practice guidelines and awareness of these guidelines in the institution can provide a basis for blood utilization audits, which are a key component to improving blood utilization. A TSO/PBMC can promote use of the guidelines and assist with development of order sets that follow institution guidelines. An assessment of the blood administration process with blood bank, nursing, information technology, and others may be the impetus to improving the ordering, delivery, administration, and documentation of blood transfusion. This can lead to the standardization of blood administration by the nursing staff and improved documentation of blood transfusions.

## Blood-Center-Based Model

Blood centers throughout the country are taking a more interactive role with their hospital customers by providing a TSO employed by the blood center. The benefits to the blood center include enhancing knowledge of the community on transfusion medicine as well as strengthening the relationship between the hospital and blood center. This is valued by many hospitals as they may not be able to employ a TSO because of decreasing insurance reimbursements and attempts to control costs. The emphasis of this collaboration is to enhance PBM efforts to increase safety, improve patient care, and reduce costs.

As with a hospital-based model, there are different approaches to utilizing a TSO based in a community blood center. Each of these approaches depends on the size and needs of the community served by the blood center. One approach is for the TSO to work directly with the medical directors of the blood center, assisting them with projects, education, and data collection at the hospitals for which they provide transfusion service. With this approach, the TSO's time may be split between more than one medical director, and time is spent working in collaboration with the blood center medical director rather than directly with the hospital itself.

In another approach, the TSO serves as a consultant to the hospital, working directly with the transfusion service and nursing department to build rapport, understanding how the hospital operates on a daily basis, and assessing the needs and challenges from an outside perspective. This TSO is employed by the blood center but works in collaboration with the hospital transfusion service medical director to provide education, participate in projects, and collect data. The amount of involvement at the hospital depends on the level of authority the TSO is given. Some hospitals will need the TSO to be credentialed with a physician sponsor to collect blood utilization data, and others will allow for special privileges. In either instance, the TSO acts as the liaison between the blood center and the hospital to promote appropriate utilization of the blood components and help set up best practices (see Fig 5-3).

There are advantages and limitations to having a blood-center-based TSO. The advantage to the hospital is that often the TSO is provided as a value-added service to the blood center customer. Some blood centers may be able to add the services of the TSO to the contract with the hospital. The biggest limitations of a blood-center-based approach is that the TSO is not on site 7 days a week at the hospital. The TSO has less opportunity to merge into the culture of the hospital. Thus, the TSO may not be a familiar face to the clinical staff. This can be overcome by creating articles and information for staff newsletters, and introductions and participation in various staff and management meetings to explain the role of a TSO, and what the TSO is and can do for their hospital. Slapak, Fredrich, and Wagner[5] describe three different approaches in which a

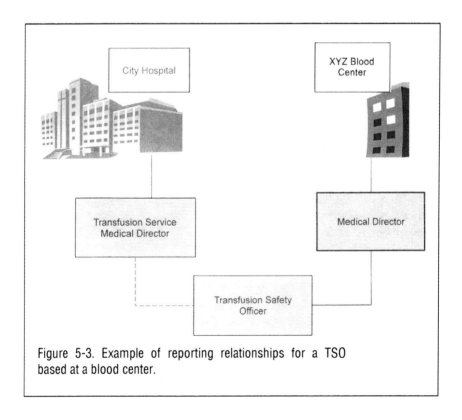

Figure 5-3. Example of reporting relationships for a TSO based at a blood center.

blood center TSO is utilized. In each approach the TSO serves as the clinical resource to the hospital and offers an extension of the blood center expertise.

## Professional Background

Which health-care professional is the ideal candidate for a TSO/PBMC? Health-care professionals all have different skills, strengths, limitations, and gaps in education that will need to be addressed to optimize the candidate's ability to perform the role. The model chosen for the institution, the position description, and the program goals will guide the decision and determine which health-care professional is most appropriate. This section discusses three possible health-care professionals, but there may be other professionals who could also be ideal candidates.[6,7]

Registered nurses are generally comfortable interacting and communicating with a variety of patients, families, and other health-care professionals. Nurses have a strong sense of how the entire hospital functions, from hospital administration to housekeeping and maintenance. The nurse's perspective of patient care is to care for the patient as a whole— the current clinical problems, the patient's and the family's goal for the care, the professionals providing the care, and what is needed to enhance the patient experience. Nurses see themselves as coordinators of all the care being provided to patients. They have a strong knowledge base of a variety of clinical conditions, the treatments available, and blood component administration, but they may lack in-depth knowledge about the actual make-up of the blood components and the testing required in the hospital blood bank. The knowledge needed about blood components, testing processes, and regulatory requirements can be acquired by having a nurse spend some concentrated time in the transfusion service, following samples from order to collection to test result.

Medical laboratory scientists (formerly termed medical technologists) have a strong knowledge base in the laboratory itself and about blood banking. They generally tend to be process-oriented and task-oriented. Due to their role, they have a strong technical and analytical focus. They are familiar with regulatory compliance and quality assurance processes within the laboratory and sometimes within the hospital as well. Medical laboratory scientists, by the nature of their jobs, may not routinely interact with individuals outside the laboratory. They are often not as familiar with the patients' clinical conditions that require a blood transfusion. Acquiring knowledge about the clinical conditions of patients who may require transfusions and learning about the procedure for administration of blood, the equipment needed, and how the documentation is completed will likely be needed. Medical laboratory scientists possess a wealth of information about blood components and compatibility, and test result interpretation that can be tapped into by others within the hospital.

Perfusionists have excellent working knowledge about the operating room (OR) arena. They are generally knowledgeable about blood recovery, acute normovolemic hemodilution, cardiac bypass circuitry, and other OR-based equipment, and blood use within the OR. They may or may not have actual blood administration experience. They may have a more narrow view of the hospital itself as they are based solely within the confines of the OR. This could result in limited clinical experience other than the OR. Depending on their personality, perfusionists may have good communication and people skills within their repertoire. Patient blood management (but not necessarily transfusion safety) may be part of a perfusionist education program. Perfusionists may need to learn the procedure for blood administration and required documentation. In addition, they will likely need to gain knowledge about the hospital transfusion service functions such as understanding of testing and preparing blood components for transfusion.

Whichever health-care professional is selected to fill the position of a TSO or PBMC, the person needs to fit the vision, culture, and needs of the institution. The goals of the institution for improving patient safety are the basis for the TSO/PBMC position. At times, when seeking a person to fill the role of a TSO/PBMC, the "perfect" candidate is already employed at the institution. The candidate may be a staff nurse or medical laboratory scientist with a strong interest in safer blood transfusion, improving patient outcomes, or reducing blood use. However, such a candidate may need to be coaxed to embark on this new position with new and unfamiliar responsibilities within their institution. The supervisor of the TSO/PBMC may, in this instance, have to mentor the leadership skills of the new TSO/PBMC. Any gaps in knowledge and skills will need to be identified and a plan created to enhance that person's knowledge to allow him or her to be successful in the new role.

Creating opportunities to build a network of other TSOs or PBMCs can facilitate the learning of a TSO/PBMC. If possible, visits with others in a similiar position can help. Attendance at national meetings, participation in TSO work groups, and e-mail contacts all help the new TSO develop the knowledge and confidence to be a leader.

## Desired Skills and Abilities

Whether working in a hospital-based or blood center-based environment, TSOs needs certain skills that will enable them to provide education, assist with process improvements, and analyze blood usage—all of which will lead to better patient outcomes. Personality characteristics of a successful TSO/PBMC include self-confidence, persistence or tenacity, excellent communication skills, good presentation and organizational skills, and the "fit" with the organization. Oftentimes a TSO/PBMC is the sole person responsible for transfusion safety or PBM for the organization, and may need to seek out mentors, resources, and contacts within the organization. Thus, self-confidence and persistence help this person to pursue the goals of the program. Candidates also need to educate themselves about all aspects of the transfusion process, particularly from blood component arrival at the hospital through administration of the unit(s) to the patient. Time spent in the transfusion service and with physicians interested in PBM may enhance the abilities of the TSO/PBMC.

Interaction with a variety of health-care professionals, patients, and families is a major job responsibility. Currently, the position of a TSO or PBMC is not widely known because few hospitals or blood centers have these employees. To promote the message to health-care professionals, TSOs and PBMCs must be able to succinctly explain their role. Many other businesses refer to this type of explanation as an "elevator speech."[8] The development and use of an "elevator speech" to explain what a TSO does or PBM in general can be a useful tool. According to Toastmasters International,[8] the most important sentence of an elevator speech is to describe the position as a solution to a problem faced by the institution. The ability to explain PBM and all of its components, in terms that patients and families can understand, is crucial to compliance with prescribed treatments. This also promotes the message of transfusion safety and improved patient care as a valued mission of the institution.

Another needed skill for TSO/PBMCs is project management. By definition, project management is "a set of tools, techniques, and knowledge that, when applied, produce improved results."[9] By design, project management tools are meant to be collaborative in nature, to be useful for a variety of projects, and to create results that meet the customer needs. Project management is a process that includes:
- Creation of a project charter and project plan.
- Management of the project team.
- Determining the project scope, timeline or schedule, and budget.

- Deciding which tools will be most effective [failure mode and effects analysis (FMEA), plan-do-study-act (PDSA), value stream mapping or other LEAN tools] to assess the project.
- Executing the plan.
- Evaluating and planning for sustainability.

A project generally consists of four phases, all of which can be under the leadership of a TSO or PBMC. Initiation is the beginning of the process and includes development of the scope of the project, goals, and any constraints or limitations. This is documented in the charter of the project. During the planning phase, team members are selected, the scope is more precisely defined, the risks are assessed, and needed resources are requested. Execution is the result of all the planning and preparation of the team. The deliverables are created, metrics are established, and all issues are addressed. Communication is an essential part of execution. Finally, the project is evaluated to determine whether the goal was met, the customer was satisfied, and what lessons were learned in the process. A final summation or report is written during the final phase of the project.[9] TSOs and PBMCs become involved in many projects surrounding transfusion safety, blood utilization, and patient blood management. To manage projects successfully, these positions require a working knowledge base of project management, leadership skills, and team management.

Transfusion safety and PBM are initiatives coming to the forefront of health care. Several models and types of health-care professionals in the role of TSO were described within this chapter. An organization can opt for either a blood center-based or hospital-based model, either of which will have an impact on patient outcomes, workload of staff, and cost of health care. Organizational culture and strategic goals will determine the model and expectations of the role. Awareness of the TSO/PBMC positions and the importance of the role within an institution will help increase these efforts. Without a position or program that focuses on these areas, hospitals may continue to struggle to make transfusion safer and optimize blood usage while facing economic pressure in the ever changing health-care environment.

## References

1. McGuiness Slapak C. Survey conducted and results presented at Nursing II: Patient Blood Management and Transfusion Safety Workshop. AABB Annual Meeting and CTTXPO, Boston, MA. October 7, 2012.

2. Lencioni P. Silos, politics, and turf wars. Hoboken, NJ: Jossey-Bass Publishing, 2006.
3. Brooks JP. Reengineering transfusion and cellular therapy processes hospitalwide: Ensuring the safe utilization of blood products. Transfusion 2005;45(Supp):159S-71S.
4. Adams KW, Weiss K, Tolich DJ. Blood transfusion: The patient's experience. Am J Nurs 2011;111(9):24-30.
5. Slapak C, Fredrich N, Wagner J. Transfusion safety: Is this the business of blood centers? JBSM 2011;51:2767-71.
6. When professions meet: Bridging the gap between laboratory and nursing. 2012 AABB Audio Conference Series. July 11, 2012. [Available at http://www.aabb.org/events/audioconferences/Pages/12descriptions.aspx#0711 (accessed September 16, 2013).]
7. Lore N. The pathfinder: How to choose or change your career for a lifetime of satisfaction and success. Simon & Schuster New York 2011.
8. Clapp C. The elevator speech. Rancho Santa Margarita, CA: Toastmasters International, October 2011. [Available at http://magazines.toastmasters.org/display_article.php?id829814 (accessed August 19, 2013).]
9. Martin P, Tate K. Getting started in project management. Hoboken, NJ: Wiley & Sons, 2001.

In: Johnson ST, Puca KE, eds.
*Transfusion Medicine's Emerging Positions: Transfusion Safety
Officers and Patient Blood Management Coordinators*
Bethesda, MD: AABB Press, 2013

# 6

# *Training for a Transfusion Safety Officer*

MARY TOWNSEND, MD, AND
HOUSTON NGUYEN, MT(ASCP)

AS HEALTH-CARE INSTITUTIONS AROUND THE UNITED States begin to advance the quality of their transfusion services through the employment of a transfusion safety officer (TSO), they may find it challenging to recruit the best candidate and to effectively train that individual. In contrast to the TSO role internationally, the position of TSO is in its infancy in the United States. For most employers, the logical first step in determining methods to train TSOs is to seek historically successful models.

## TSO Training Around the World

In 2011, members of the Dutch national hemovigilance platform conducted an international survey among TSOs. There were 151 responses from 27 countries. Participants were asked to identify specialized training they received as a TSO or equivalent. These responses demonstrate that countries with a history of transfusion safety specialists have

Mary Townsend, MD, Senior Medical Director, Blood Systems, Inc., and Houston Nguyen, MT(ASCP), Transfusion Safety Officer, Blood Systems, Inc., Scottsdale, Arizona
The authors have disclosed no conflicts of interest.

developed educational programs and certifications to prepare their employees in this field (see Table 6-1).[1]

In the same survey, 97% noted that their initial training was performed in an on-the-job setting with another TSO, and the same percentage of participants relied on national guidelines in their daily work. One can conclude from this information that through national transfusion guidelines and years of TSO practice, some nations have established an array of nationally recognized resources and internal support to adequately prepare their TSOs. Three examples are described below.

**Australia**

The Graduate Certificate in Transfusion Practice is a 1-year long online program offered by The Melbourne School of Nursing.[2] This program was developed in partnership with Blood Service, Australia's national blood provider, and consists of four courses: Fundamentals in Transfusion Practice, Quality within Transfusion Practice, Transfusion Practice-Advanced Concepts, and Transfusion Specialty Practice. This postgraduate program is intended to provide students with the skills and knowledge to serve as a specialist in transfusion practice.

### Table 6-1. Education for Transfusion Safety Officers[1]

| Education Method | Country |
| --- | --- |
| Transfusion awareness training/diploma in transfusion medicine | United Kingdom |
| *Bloody Easy* online courses | Canada |
| N 59AA graduate certificate in transfusion practice | Australia |
| Diplome universitaire de transfusion sanguine | France |
| In-house training at job introduction | Finland |
| Postmarketing surveillance | Japan |
| Specialised source in blood transfusion medicine | China |
| Module three: Professional development specialist | Ireland |
| Three modules at Dublin City University (nurse) | Malta |
| European Hemovigilance Network/International Hemovigilance Network | Multiple respondents |
| TRIP workshops, Sanguin seminars | The Netherlands |

Fundamentals in Transfusion Practice is an introduction to the basic elements of transfusion. Students are taught basic hematology and the transfusion process from vein to vein. Quality within Transfusion Practice covers quality policies and risk management related to collection and posttransfusion management of blood components. Advanced Concepts of Transfusion Practice discusses in detail transfusion-transmitted infections, clinical guidelines for the use of blood components, specialized blood components, and individual coagulation factor replacements. This course also identifies alternatives to blood transfusion. Transfusion Specialty Practice helps the students transition from theoretical concepts to applied knowledge. This last phase of the curriculum engages the student in practical exercises, such as developing patient education on blood transfusion and devising auditing tools on aspects of transfusion practice.

Such a focused education program adequately prepares TSOs to help hospitals meet the national standards in transfusion practice.

## Canada

The Ontario Regional Blood Coordinating Network offers an electronic learning tool called *Bloody Easy*.[3] This tool is available to health professionals seeking to enhance their knowledge of blood transfusions and the alternatives. Canadian TSOs also can register with www.transfusionsafety.ca to join a large community of professionals involved in transfusion medicine. This forum provides TSOs with the opportunity to share best practices and identify hurdles in their workplace. Details on the Canadian experience are found in Chapter 8.

## United States

In recent years, the number of TSOs has grown in the United States because of emerging studies highlighting risks of inappropriate use of blood components and interest in reducing costs associated with transfusion medicine. Because the initiative is in its infancy, hospital recruiters may find it difficult to identify a suitable candidate with adequate training and education to perform the expected tasks. With the scarcity of either trained TSOs or a formal training program, most early TSOs were recruited internally from within their hospital and asked to serve in this new role, largely relying on on-the-job training. A survey was conducted in 2012 to capture a snapshot of the current Transfusion Safety/Blood Management programs in the United States, Canada, and other countries. Coordinators were asked how they were trained to perform their role (Table 6-2).[4] Only 8 of 95 survey respondents indicated they had received education from a formal TSO orientation program. In the same survey, respondents indicated the location of their program. Of those 108 programs, 35 were located in the United States, 67 were located in Canada, and 6 were located in other countries including India, England, Argentina, and Australia (see Table 6-3). Judging by these results and the aforementioned availability of education outside of the United States, it is safe to conclude most individuals participating in the survey from the United States received little, if any, formal education.

TSOs in the United States have been able to seek training through online materials, self-training from transfusion literature and clinical studies, attendance at annual conferences, and networking with other TSOs. Various organizations have acknowledged this gap in education and are developing offerings to current TSOs, individuals aspiring to become TSOs, and individuals looking to hire and train TSOs. Consulting firms offer on-the-job training for TSOs or TSO equivalents while simultaneously implementing a patient blood management (PBM) program at the

## Table 6-2. TSO Training Methods Identified by Survey Respondents[4]

| Training Methods Experienced by Respondents | Response Percent | Response Count |
|---|---|---|
| Initial training in nursing or laboratory science PLUS years of experience in transfusion service/ blood management | 65% | 62 |
| Formal TSO orientation program | 8% | 8 |
| Attendance at national meetings such as AABB, SABM | 40% | 38 |
| Networking with other TSO/blood management managers | 53% | 50 |
| Other (eg, self-study, on-the-job training) | 22% | 21 |
| | answered question | 95 |
| | skipped question | 13 |

**Table 6-3. Locations of TSO Programs Identified by Survey Respondents[4]**

| Location | Response Percent | Response Count |
|---|---|---|
| United States | 32% | 35 |
| Canada | 62% | 67 |
| Other | 6% | 6 |
| Total Programs | | 108 |

hospital. Some organizations have taken the approach of offering comprehensive TSO training with ongoing support for the students.

## Curriculum

The role of the TSO was internationally developed, shaped, and honed over roughly a decade outside any formal training program. Thus, no established curriculum has been available until recently, when formal programs were developed in Europe and Australia. To confound the problem further, TSOs come from divergent backgrounds including clinical disciplines (nurses, physician assistants, perfusionists, among others) and nonclinical disciplines [medical laboratory scientists (medical technologists), and quality specialists]. Given the divergent backgrounds of transfusion practitioners, one of the primary challenges of a formal curriculum is to develop a common language or vocabulary. Although nurses are trained and experienced in the process of transfusing blood components and handling reactions, they sometimes lack knowledge regarding the various types of testing done on blood, the nuances of appropriateness of transfusion, and familiarity with data collection and analysis needed to drive a PBM program. Conversely, medical laboratory scientists are familiar with the testing and crossmatching of blood components and the complexities of blood group antigens, but generally lack specific understanding of the clinical aspects of patient care, the implications and applications of data management, or the nuances involved in education of and communication with clinicians.[5] (See Chapter 4 for more detail.)

This diversity of backgrounds provides a challenge in identifying knowledge gaps to be addressed during the training period. Without a formal training program, individuals pursuing a career as a TSO have often needed to recognize and fill those gaps for themselves.

## Elements of a TSO Curriculum

Elements of the TSO curriculum include topics related to theory (the knowledge base) as well as to skills (the practical base). The TSO serves many roles within his or her hospital, and in many cases may be the most knowledgeable person in the hospital with regard to transfusion medicine issues and questions. In order to be the Subject Matter Expert (SME), the TSO should have a wide knowledge base spanning a diversity of topics from screening, collecting, testing, and distributing blood through to the ultimate transfusion of the blood component to the recipient, including an indefinite period following transfusion during which an adverse event could develop. Furthermore, as the hospital transfusion SME, the TSO should become related to PBM and the alternatives to transfusion therapy.

## Blood Collection Facility Essentials

A working knowledge of the activities that take place at the blood collection facility is essential to the TSO. The various steps taken at the blood collection facility—from donor screening, collection, and testing through manufacture and distribution—all contribute to blood safety.[6]

### Donor Screening

Donor screening takes place in a confidential environment with the dual purpose of identifying donors who might pose harm to themselves by donating (because of an underlying medical condition) and of identifying donors who might pose a risk to the recipient (because of a risk of a communicable disease or use of a potentially harmful medication). Although blood centers do an admirable job of screening out potentially risky donors, neither the process nor the donor's memory is perfect, and at times ineligible donors donate blood. It is important for TSOs to be familiar with the various conditions for donor deferral because it is inevitable that at some point they will have to deal with notification from their blood supplier alerting them to the distribution of a blood component inadvertently collected from an ineligible donor. A working knowledge of donor eligibility and deferral criteria enable the TSO to communicate knowledgeably with the physician(s), risk management department, or patient without eliciting undue alarm.

## Collection

Likewise, blood centers perform a number of steps during the collection of blood that incrementally reduce risk. Bacterial contamination of the component is reduced through the use of validated arm scrub materials and processes and through the use of a collection pouch that diverts the initial small volume of blood, including the potentially contaminated skin plug, for use in required testing. In some cases, the collection process may include a leukocyte reduction step or, in the case of automated collections, this may be performed concurrently by the collection device.

## Component Manufacturing

Separation of blood into its components includes many steps to ensure or enhance the safety of the unit. For components that were not leukocyte-reduced during the collection process, this step is usually performed at some point during the separation process. When indicated, additional processing to enhance the safety of blood includes irradiation, freezing and deglycerolizing, and washing.

## Testing

Of all the interventions associated with the increased safety of blood, none is so apparent as the extensive testing that occurs before release. As a resource to both patients and clinical staff, it is incumbent upon the TSO to be familiar with the testing performed both in the blood collection facility and in the hospital blood bank, and to recognize the implications of the many complex test algorithms and results. This applies both to tests for infectious agents as well as for the many tests performed for other reasons. Additional testing includes the quality control testing of platelets to detect possible bacterial contamination. A thorough working knowledge of the tests and significance of results is important, because the TSO will likely be involved with the inevitable product recalls and withdrawals as well as look-back notifications from the blood provider.

Additional testing of concern to the physician, and ultimately to patient care, includes tests performed by the immunohematology reference laboratory, a service often made available by the blood provider, including testing for antibodies against specific red cell antigens to red cells, leukocytes, neutrophils, or platelets.

The sum total of these tests, together with their implications on patient management and care, constitutes but one example of the complexities that challenge the TSO as he or she acts as the bridge connecting the blood provider, transfusion service, physician, nursing staff, and patient in the continuous quality cycle of patient safety.[7]

## Quality Essentials

For TSOs working in the hospital setting, there will always be a focus on process improvement and quality patient care. Understanding how a quality strategy fits together cohesively with the various hospital departments can be very challenging. The TSO must first recognize what elements or fundamentals comprise the quality system in his or her organization. There are generally 10 quality system essentials that make up the quality system for the transfusion service/blood bank and have an impact on patient testing and blood administration. The goal is to ensure that the process of patient care—including the decision to transfuse, processing of the blood component, and appropriate administration of the unit for an expected benefit—falls under these established essentials. A quality monitoring function is required for quality assessment by regulatory agencies such as the Food and Drug Administration (FDA) and the Centers for Medicare and Medicaid Services (CMS) as well as the following groups that offer voluntary accreditation:

- AABB
- College of American Pathologists
- Committee on Laboratory Accreditation
- Det Norske Veritas
- The Joint Commission

The TSO completing a training curriculum should be familiar with the quality systems for the blood provider, the transfusion service/blood bank, the clinical departments, and the hospital at large as well as how he or she will interact with each.

## Risks of Blood Transfusion

### Infectious Risks

No doubt for the lay person, and perhaps for most medical professionals as well, the single most important recognized risk of a blood transfusion is the transmission of an infectious disease, with the specter of human immunodeficiency virus (HIV) and hepatitis foremost. Beyond these well-known pathogens lie a number of other viruses, bacteria, parasites, and even prions that are proven or potential passengers suspected of being transmitted in blood. The well-trained TSO should be familiar with the relative risks of transfusion-transmitted diseases as well as everyday risks to which the physician and patient can relate. The concept of residual risk is important in that it reflects the risk remaining after interventions such as donor screening, testing, leukocyte reduction, and others are applied.

*Noninfectious Risks*

Although infectious risks of transfusion garner attention by the public, the press, and even medical professionals, transfusion medicine professionals have raised the awareness of the noninfectious adverse outcomes of transfusion. Some of the interest in patient blood management has grown out of the realization that although many risks of blood transfusion can be reduced, all risks cannot be eliminated. Again, the TSO should be aware of the more frequent, and in some cases lethal, risks of transfusion and of the relative rate of each (up to 4 logs greater) in comparison to infectious risks and to familiar, everyday risks. Furthermore, conventional wisdom holds that while infectious risks are often the focus of the blood provider, noninfectious risks are within the purview of the hospital. Recognition of noninfectious outcomes is made either while the recipient is in the hospital or sometime after discharge.

**Blood Banking/Transfusion Medicine Essentials**

Just as transfusion professionals need a working knowledge of infectious disease and other tests performed by the blood provider and/or an immunohematology reference laboratory, they also need to be able to speak the language of the blood bank technologist in what is likely to be daily communication. Even for TSOs coming from a laboratory background, the limited amount of blood bank training they had may have long faded, unless they have worked actively to maintain their knowledge and keep up in the rapidly progressing field of transfusion medicine. For TSOs coming from a clinical background, although they may have ordered blood typing and crossmatching hundreds of times, they may have little or no notion of what the testing involves and how complex the problem becomes once the antibody screen tests positive for an unexpected antibody(ies). Again, the goal is not an in-depth working knowledge of the complexities of the field of immunohematology, but the development of a common vocabulary and an appreciation for the all the steps that have to happen and "go right" in order to provide the right product for the right patient at the right time. In general TSOs should have a working understanding of basic testing—including ABO and Rh typing, antibody screen, and crossmatch—as well as some of the more common, sophisticated issues such as provision of antigen-negative components, selection of blood for emergencies and for special clinical situations (sickle cell disease, transplantation, hemolytic disease of the fetus and newborn, neonatal immune thrombocytopenia), and the workup of a transfusion reaction.

## Transfusion Administration Essentials

Just as the TSO coming from a clinical background may need remedial training in order to speak the language of his or her laboratory peer, the TSO coming from the laboratory will likely need remedial training to facilitate clear communication with the nursing and clinical staff with whom he or she will have daily contact. Although some of the topics may seem painfully simple, training in skills such as proper specimen collection, needle bore and tubing size selection, and appropriate transfusion rate all contribute to patient safety.

## Transfusion Reactions

Ideally, the TSO should be contacted every time a transfusion reaction is suspected, and the earlier the better. However, the process of adverse transfusion event recognition begins long before the blood ever starts down through the tubing into the patient's vein. It starts with the education of the clinical nursing and physician staff about the spectrum of adverse events with emphasis on prompt recognition, treatment, workup, and reporting. There may be no one more qualified to perform this vital education than the knowledgeable TSO. Thus, TSO training should cover all aspects of transfusion reactions in depth, including the following:

- Definition and description of adverse events.
- Specific signs and symptoms.
- Pathophysiology, when known.
- Treatment.
- Workup.
- Reporting and tracking (hemovigilance).

Different algorithms available to assist in transfusion reaction diagnosis by categorizing reactions (as febrile/afebrile, immune/non-immune, acute/delayed) may be helpful to clinical staff who make decisions regarding treatment in urgent situations.

## Unexpected Outcomes of Transfusion

Although adverse transfusion reactions are by far the most commonly considered unexpected outcomes of transfusion, the TSO needs to be aware of other, less well-known events. These include alloimmunization with subsequent platelet refractoriness and posttransfusion purpura. Because these outcomes are removed in time from the actual transfusion event, often by weeks or months, they are often not associated with a previous transfusion. The TSO should have a thorough understanding of the pathophysiology of these events, should exercise continuous surveillance in order to recognize these events and associate them with transfusion, and should understand implications for the provision of additional blood components in the future.

# Blood Utilization and Management

Although the area of blood and transfusion safety, including transfusion reactions, has been the traditional domain of the TSO, hospitals taking more accountability for the proper use of precious—and costly—resources such as blood, are turning to PBM programs. In identifying an individual to take the lead for the organization, hospital administrators ought to turn to the most knowledgeable individual in the hospital, which in many cases is the TSO. Thus, TSO curricula should include basic grounding in the tenets of PBM.

## Appropriate Indications for Transfusion

As with any other medical intervention, the decision to transfuse a blood component should come from a thoughtful consideration of risks and benefits based on data-driven evidence. Unfortunately, transfusion therapy has too often been taken for granted as a therapeutic modality. Carefully conducted, randomized, double-blinded studies have established standards of care and best practice for many medical disciplines; however, transfusion has been a tradition-based practice wherein physicians learned much about transfusion from their residents, often decades ago, with little thought of what they are transfusing or why. Fortunately, active research into the real benefits and even more real risks of transfusion have begun to establish evidence-based guidelines for the appropriate use of blood.

The greater challenge becomes changing the habits of ordering physicians from tradition-based to evidence-based practice. In the moderate-sized hospital with no transfusion medicine trained physician on staff, the TSO may be the person most qualified to speak to the appropriateness of transfusion practice and to push changes in transfusion practice. The thoroughly trained TSO will be able to speak with authority and work with physicians to slowly bring about needed change in practice. Admittedly, appropriate indications for transfusion will continue to evolve as the results of clinical trials are published, but the professional TSO should maintain his or her proficiency through meeting attendance and keeping current with published studies.[8]

## Special Clinical Situations

With the rapid advance of technological innovations, medicine continues to increase in complexity, and the challenge of providing support with and without blood components will parallel this rise in complexity. Examples include the escalation in advances in caring for trauma patients rising out of recent decades of global conflict. Although many of the lessons learned are still considered premature or controversial, trauma surgeons are already changing how they order and transfuse blood to address the coagulopathy of trauma. Other examples include targeted transfusion products for patients with sickle cell anemia or patients undergoing stem cell transplants. TSOs need to understand the needs of special patient populations, how blood transfusion is affected, how to work with clinical colleagues to establish appropriate massive hemorrhage protocols and, when appropriate, to become an active member of the team managing these special situations.

## Alternatives to Transfusion

PBM encompasses much more than simply the concept of "bloodless surgery," but to a great extent, PBM does include avoidance of blood components when possible and safe. Over time, a number of PBM approaches have been identified. Although the use of a single intervention is rarely sufficient, the use of the right combination of pharmacologic and nonpharmacologic interventions can lead to a reduction or outright elimination of the need for blood.

***Pharmacologic Products.*** The number of pharmacologic products to prevent or reduce bleeding continues to grow and includes both biologics and pharmaceuticals that increase clotting efficacy, reduce fibrinolysis, or enhance hemoglobin production. Just as blood components provided both benefits and risks, so do all pharmacologic products. The TSO needs to be conversant regarding the specific products available on the hospital formulary, the specific indications of each product, their side effects, and relevant contraindications.

*Nonpharmacologic Products.* Nonpharmacologic approaches have been in place since the 1980s when the association with HIV and blood transfusion prompted surgeons to recommend that patients provide their own blood for surgery. Patients, in turn, insisted on having blood donated by friends and family who, in theory, were considered safer. Although the use of autologous and directed donations has appropriately declined, the use of preoperative autologous donation is still considered an option for a patient whose blood use is likely to be moderately high and who has the time to replenish his or her hemoglobin level before surgery. TSOs should be acquainted with those modalities as well as with the many other alternatives including intraoperative blood recovery, regional anesthesia, acute normovolemic hemodilution, topical sealants, and blood recovery from postoperative drainage.

*Presurgical Anemia Clinics.* One of the most logical approaches to PBM, presurgical anemia clinics, has recently gained popularity. Regardless of the setting, patients often have low hemoglobin levels before entering the hospital. A number of factors have contributed to this situation. First, patients often undergo their preoperative testing (CBC, EKG, chest xray, other) a few days before admission, and with same-day surgery some are not tested until early on the day of surgery, leaving no time to address and correct anemia. Second, with the advent of preoperative autologous donation, many patients who were not initially anemic became so after donating blood for their surgery. Finally, patients likely to undergo surgery often have underlying conditions, such as chronic inflammation, that deters normal hematopoiesis, leaving them chronically anemic. The presurgical anemia clinic functions by identifying and correcting anemia in patients with planned, elective surgery. Patients are usually referred to the clinic by their surgeons based on testing done well in advance (4 or more weeks before surgery). An important aspect is determining the source of the underlying anemia in order to diagnose any condition that should be addressed before surgery—an occult cancer, for example. Once the etiology of the underlying anemic state is addressed, the patient is treated with iron supplementation or perhaps erythropoietin to restore iron reserves. TSOs serving as patient blood management coordinators (PBMCs) can have an influential role in establishing and monitoring the function of these clinics. In order to do so, a thorough understanding is required of the pathophysiology of the most common sources of anemia, of the varied treatment modalities, and of project management skills required to pull it all off.

## Auditing

A major task, related to both the transfusion safety and PBM aspects of the TSO role, involves auditing. Auditing is not generally a skill that comes naturally; meaningful auditing is a thoughtful, structured process that is essential to the functioning of the TSO, and should be a part of the formal training curriculum. Throughout his or her day, the TSO likely audits many facets of the transfusion process. It is not an exaggeration that the bulk of meaningful information is obtained through this auditing function. Examples of audits include the following:

- Blood component infusion: to observe for adherence to transfusion policies and procedures.
- Transfusion reactions: to ascertain compliance with procedures for recognition, treatment, and reporting and to establish if underrecognition and underreporting are an issue.
- Concurrent or retrospective (chart) audits: to determine compliance with established transfusion guidelines.

## Function of the Transfusion Committee and Peer Review

Regardless of the specific structure of the transfusion committee and/or blood utilization committee within a given hospital, it is essential that the TSO play an active role within the committee. Formal training should include committee basics including structure, membership, regulatory requirements, concept of quality indicators, and essential duties.

## Other Elements of a PBM Program

In their role within the hospital PBM structure, TSOs need to be familiar with a number of other concepts or elements of PBM. These elements should be included in any formal TSO training program to provide the TSO with a basic working knowledge. Examples include the following:

- Iatrogenic blood loss: an understanding of the cause of iatrogenic blood loss through uncoordinated, random, or rote collection of blood samples for testing, especially in the intensive care and pediatric patient populations, together with possible solutions to the problem.

- Point-of-care (POC) testing: although the specific instruments available for POC testing change over time, TSOs should have a working knowledge regarding the POC products available (especially for surgical and trauma applications), the use and interpretation of tests, and the role of these instruments in a PBM program.

## Skill-Based Training

Knowledge-based training on a wide variety of tasks focused either on transfusion safety or PBM is not the full extent of training for a TSO. Although the sheer volume of the knowledge base may seem daunting, a bigger challenge may be the acquisition and/or honing of skills known as "soft skills," which enable the transfusion practitioner to perform his or her job effectively. What are soft skills? Soft skills are intangible behaviors and interpersonal attributes that enable people to interact and perform effectively within a job. Given the nature of the job and the wide variety of contacts—physicians, nurses, laboratory technologists, quality specialists, pharmacists, hospital administration, patients, risk managers, information technologists, financial officers, to mention a few—it is essential that the TSO be proficient in a number of soft skills.

Although it is not possible to offer the TSO exhaustive training in the full array of soft skills, a few are so vital to success that they should be included in formal TSO training. However, the fully functional TSO will spend his or her career honing these and a number of other special skills and techniques. A brief list of these skills includes the following:

- Effective communication.
- Meeting management.
- Problem solving.
- Public speaking.
- Team building.
- Time management.
- Project management.
- Adult education.
- Conflict resolution.

Many resources are available to assist in delivering soft skill training. However, it should be emphasized that soft skills are taught through hands-on practice using teaching techniques such as role playing, case studies, workshops, simulations, and mentoring. Ultimately, soft skills are acquired over time through practice and modeling.

## Conclusion

TSOs should be viewed by colleagues as the subject matter expert in transfusion medicine and its surrounding practices. TSOs are tasked to transform transfusion medicine from its current state of disparate processes into an evidence- and quality-based, whole-hospital system. A robust range of technical and interpersonal training and education provide the best means of preparing TSOs to bridge those gaps.

## References

1. International Society of Blood Transfusion. Successful international hemovigilance seminar, Amsterdam: ISBT, 2011. [Available at http://www.isbtweb.org/academy/academy-event-reports/2011/ (accessed August 19, 2013).]
2. University of Melbourne. Graduate certificate in transfusion practice course description. Melbourne, Australia: UoM Commercial, 2013. [Available at http://www.commercial.unimelb.edu.au/transfusionpractice/ (accessed August 19, 2013).]
3. Callum J, Lin Y, Pinkerton PH. Bloody easy 3: Blood transfusions, blood alternatives, and transfusion reactions—A guide to transfusion medicine. Ottawa, Canada: Ontario Regional Blood Coordinating Network, 2011. [Available at http://www.transfusionmedicine.ca/resources/links/textbooks-handbooks/bloody-easy-2-blood-transfusions-blood-alternatives-and-transfus (accessed September 16, 2013).]
4. McGuinness-Slapak C. Survey conducted and results presented at Nursing II: Patient Blood Management and Transfusion Safety Workshop. AABB Annual Meeting and CTTXPO, Boston, MA. October 7, 2012.
5. Dzik WH, Corwin H, Goodnough LT, et al. Patient safety and blood transfusion: New solutions. Transfus Med Rev 2003;17:169-80.
6. Slapak C, Fredrich N, Wagner J. Transfusion safety: Is this the business of blood centers? Transfusion 2011;51(12pt2):2767-71.
7. America's Blood Centers. Transfusion safety officers can enhance blood safety, says FDA. ABC Newsletter. 2011;7:4-5.
8. Improving the safety of the blood transfusion process. Pennsylvania Patient Safety Advisory 2010;7(2):33. [Available at http://patientsafetyauthority.org/ADVISORIES/AdvisoryLibrary/2010/Jun7(2)/Pages/33.aspx (accessed September 17, 2013).]

In: Johnson ST, Puca KE, eds.
*Transfusion Medicine's Emerging Positions: Transfusion Safety
Officers and Patient Blood Management Coordinators*
Bethesda, MD: AABB Press, 2013

# 7

# *Building a Business Case*

## JOSEPH THOMAS, RN, BSN, AND
## COLLEEN McGUINNESS SLAPAK, MS, MT(ASCP)SBB

THE FIRST SEVERAL CHAPTERS OF THIS BOOK HAVE established the clinical need for improved transfusion safety and strategies to optimize safety, reviewed the roles of transfusion safety officers (TSOs) and patient blood management coordinators (PBMCs), described various models and programs, and investigated education and training recommendations for staff. This chapter provides an extensive overview of successful business case development. Additionally, this discussion identifies the clinical and financial opportunities that can result from implementing a PBM and transfusion safety program. Although all of the principles in this chapter can be applied in support of developing a comprehensive blood management program, the discussion will focus on building the business case for the existence of a TSO/PBMC position.

Joseph Thomas, RN, BSN, Senior Transfusion Safety Nurse Consultant, Strategic Healthcare Group, LLC, Indianapolis, Indiana; and Colleen McGuinness Slapak, MS, MT(ASCP)SBB, Transfusion Safety Director, Community Blood Center/Community Tissue Service, Dayton, Ohio

The authors have disclosed no conflicts of interest.

# First Steps

## What Is a Business Case and Why Do I Need One?

A business case captures the reasoning of why a business (eg, hospital, blood center) should invest in a project. It is often presented in a well-structured written document, but may also come in the form of a verbal argument or presentation. The logic of the business case is that, whenever resources such as money or time are consumed, they should be in support of a specific business need. A compelling business case adequately captures both the quantifiable and unquantifiable characteristics of a proposed project. A well-designed business case defines a current problem, proposes a solution, states the resources associated with implementation of the solution, and calculates the return on investment (ROI) that could potentially be realized if implementation is successful.

## What Is the Difference Between a Business Case and a Business Plan?

The difference between a business case and a business plan is the scope and the purpose. A business case presents the argument for initiating a project. A business plan provides the implementation road map needed to execute the project and deliver the expected ROI. Depending upon the project, a business case may contain enough detail for implementation or may then be expanded into a more detailed business plan.

## How Do I Get Started?

It is important to appreciate that developing a business case may take a significant amount of time and resources. It may require an extensive gap analysis to provide the rationale for the case. The case should demonstrate a thorough evaluation, including the needs assessment, costs, and risks associated with the plan; technical and logistic aspects; ROI estimates; and metrics that will be monitored to track and measure progress.

Various templates are available to assist in the development of a business case. There are no set rules on the name of the elements, the order of elements, or the length of the document, as long as the information provided is clear and concise, allowing for a decision to be made. The following business case elements are commonly included:
- Executive Summary.
- Problem Statement.
- Proposed Solution.

- Project Description.
- Financial Analysis.
- Conclusion and Recommendations.
- Supporting Materials.

The following discussion carefully reviews most of the business case elements listed above. However, it is important to determine first if one should invest the time and resources necessary even to build the business case. This involves assurance that the proposal aligns with the hospital or blood center's strategic goals and mission. If so, then one should define and clarify the proposal's goals, collect the supporting data, estimate costs and potential funding, and review the case to determine project feasibility. If the project will be considered by the executive team, drafting of the business case can begin.

The case should anticipate questions and concerns that will be raised by the executives and proactively address them as much as possible. In general, the business case should be able to explain "who, what, when, where, how, and why." One example could be the following:

*Example: Establishing a Transfusion Safety Officer/Patient Blood Management Coordinator position:*

- What will this position do to solve issues and opportunities identified in the gap analysis?
- Why is this specific position needed and does it need to be a new hire or can it be absorbed by existing personnel?
- Who would fill the position and what is the job description?
- When can the position be filled?
- Where will this position reside (cost center) and to which department will it report?
- How much time and money will be required to realize the benefits defined?

## Business Case Elements

### Executive Summary

The executive summary is a condensed version of the business case, written so that it succinctly presents all key elements of the case within one or two pages. Some refer to the executive summary as the "2-minute drill"—whereby the case is effectively communicated and the request justified in a short time. Thus, the executive summary demands a different approach to writing than the rest of the proposal, one that balances efficient delivery of key information with a persuasive, well-substantiated delivery. Above all, the executive summary should demonstrate a clear understanding of the hospital or blood center's needs. A good way to do this is to focus on the ROI, deliverables, and measurable outcomes. The most critical information should appear in the first couple of paragraphs. A strong executive summary is crafted with the audience firmly in mind: hospital executives who are interested in bottom-line deliverables, not details. To reach this audience, an executive summary should do three things: identify the problem, recommend a solution, and provide substantiation.

### Establish the Need or Identify the Problem

This may be more challenging than first appears. With all of the competing financial and safety issues that hospitals face today, leadership needs to be convinced that this is a problem worth addressing. In the case of the TSO it will be important to create a sense of urgency based on a carefully conducted gap analysis involving both safety and financial aspects.

* Safety/Quality/Compliance opportunity—unnecessary or excessive ordering of blood components, patient safety gaps during blood administration and patient monitoring (patient identification, vital signs, unrecognized/unreported adverse events), near-misses or sentinel events related to blood administration.
* Financial opportunity—blood utilization savings based on benchmarks or blood utilization review assessment, blood component wastage.

*Recommend the Solution and Explain Its Value*

The recommendation should be firm and clear. The quantifiable value of the solution should be explained—not so much what the solution is, but what the impact of the recommended solution will be. Rather than technical details, the summary should include statements such as "The TSO position will decrease unnecessary blood utilization and reduce the hospital's blood budget by XX%." The value proposition is often financial but may be more focused on patient safety or compliance issues.

*Provide Substantiation*

The summary should give the key reasons why the TSO is the right solution for the organization. Included in this section are examples or case studies of how other hospital PBM programs have utilized TSOs or

PBMCs to significantly improve PBM and transfusion safety and thus improve patient outcomes.

## The Problem Statement

The problem statement clearly defines the reason for developing the business case and provides a vision for moving forward. This section of the document provides background information on why the problem exists and its current impact on the organization.[1] It may also include analysis and projections about potential adverse issues if the current problem continues. After someone reads the problem statement, they should have a strong idea of the nature of the opportunity, as well as a plan to address this opportunity. A good problem statement may have the following items:

- What the problem is.
- Where it is occurring.
- When it occurred.
- The extent of the problem.
- How one knows it is a problem.

In the case of a TSO position, an example could be as follows:
- *What the problem is:* Excessive and/or inappropriate blood utilization and inadequate blood utilization oversight.
- *Where the problem occurs:* All in-patient and out-patient hospital settings where blood is transfused.
- *When the problem occurred:* Gap analysis (or benchmark) of blood utilization in FY2012.
- *Extent of the problem:* If extrapolated, the % of transfusions ordered outside of hospital evidence-based guidelines result in XX unnecessary transfusions and $XX in hospital acquisition costs (benchmark comparison may be used if available).
- *How to determine it is a problem:* The % of transfusion orders that are outside of hospital guidelines and $XX in unnecessary acquisition expenditures are significantly higher than other health system hospitals (benchmark comparison may be used if available).

## The Proposed Solution

The proposed solution identifies recommended solutions to address the issues defined in the problem statement. Alternatives to the recommended solution should also be included to allow consideration of all viable options. Justification with supporting information should be included to explain why the recommended solution is the preferred one. For example:

- *Proposed Solution:* Establishing a TSO/PBMC (1 FTE) in the quality department to provide ownership of the PBM program, be accountable for reducing unnecessary blood use, and to improve transfusion safety for all patients.
- *Proposed Solution Alternative:* Establishing a TSO/PBMC (0.4-0.6 FTE) in the quality department to provide ownership of the PBM program, be accountable for reducing unnecessary blood use, and to improve transfusion safety for cardiac and orthopedic surgery patients.

## The Project Description

The project description provides details on how the proposed solution will be successfully implemented. It begins with a high-level review of the project that describes how to address the defined business problem, followed by a listing of the business goals and how they will be addressed in the project. Also included should be an explanation of the methods to be used to measure performance based on resources used or services provided. It is important to include a projected budget as well as a projected timeline with milestones and target completion dates.

## The Financial Analysis

The financial analysis element evaluates the costs and benefits of all solutions proposed, including the possibility of no action being taken. Assistance from the accounting department staff on completing a cost/benefit analysis of the project is highly recommended. Their assistance can help identify direct costs (eg, labor, supplies) and indirect costs (eg, overhead) that should be accounted for in the project. They may also have historical information and access to industry standards (eg, salary, benefits) that may be useful.

A cost/benefit analysis evaluates all potential costs and revenues that may occur during the project to determine if the project is financially feasible. The potential costs of a project should include all the processes that will be affected. For example, the cost analysis for implementation of a TSO position to reduce the overuse of blood transfusion should include not only the cost of blood components themselves, but also the cost of testing and preparing the blood for transfusion, administering and monitoring the transfusion, and managing potential adverse events.[2,3]

ROI is a performance measure used to evaluate the efficiency of an investment. A basic calculation of ROI is the gain from the investment minus the cost of the investment, divided by the cost of the investment.[4] The ROI is commonly expressed as a percentage. Using the example of implementing a TSO position to reduce overuse of blood transfusions, the cost of investment is the direct and indirect cost of implementing the position. If the proposed solution anticipates a 5% reduction in red cell transfusions within a specified time frame, then the gain in investment is the predicted savings based on historical numbers.

Charts and graphs are recommended whenever possible to present data. Visual prompts illustrate key points more effectively than text and tables. All data and calculations should be double-checked for accuracy. Supporting detail or references should be available in case the analysis is questioned when presented.

## The Conclusion and Recommendation

The conclusion and recommendations section closes the business case by restating the problem, identifying the recommended solution, and highlighting key points. It is important to include the ROI if the recommended solution is implemented as well as the other benefits of implementation and the risks if nothing is done. The message that should be conveyed to the executive audience is "we need to move forward" on this project.

## Summary

A business case template has been included as Appendix 7-1. The authors of this chapter recommend review of this template as well as others to find the format that fits best. Readers who have never written a business case before are welcome to use the format of the template provided. Key points to remember include: be succinct, justify goals, provide evidence, and double-check all numbers.

## References

1. Corvelay A. How to write a problem statement for business. Santa Monica, CA: Demand Media, 1999-2013 [Available at http://www.ehow.com/how_6613061_write-problem-statement-business.html#ixzz2Pn6HEzWK (accessed August 7, 2013).]

2. Shander A, Hofmann A, Ozawa S, et al. Activity-based costs of blood transfusion in surgical patients at four hospitals. Transfusion 2010;50:753-65.

3. Hannon TJ, Gjerde KP. The contemporary economics of transfusion. In: Spiess BD, Spence RK, Shander A, eds. Perioperative transfusion medicine. 2nd ed. Philadelphia: Lippincott Williams & Wilkins, 2005:13-38.

4. Return on investment. Westlake Village, CA: ValueClick, 2013. [Available at: http://www.investopedia.com/terms/r/returnoninvestment.asp#axzz2M1J6P Jtv (accessed August 7, 2013).]

## Appendix 7-1. Transfusion Safety Officer Business Proposal*

### Title of Project: Transfusion Safety Officer Position

#### Executive Summary

Blood transfusion has become the most common in-patient procedure at HOSPITAL (12,000 blood component transfusions/year) while over the past 10 years the acquisition cost for blood components has more than doubled ($2,500,000/year with associated transfusion costs estimated at $8M - $14M). In addition, audits have revealed that as many as 38% of blood components at HOSPITAL are ordered and administered outside of evidence-based guidelines. Several other clinical knowledge and performance gaps related to transfusion safety have been identified throughout the hospital, creating opportunities for medicolegal risk and patient adverse events. When this precious, scarce, and expensive resource is used inappropriately or excessively, it results in avoidable patient harm. A coordinated hospital approach is necessary to successfully achieve the goal of improved patient outcomes. By establishing a comprehensive patient blood management (PBM) program with a dedicated Transfusion Safety Officer (TSO) to provide ownership and accountability, HOSPITAL has the opportunity to improve clinical outcomes, reduce patient harm, and save an estimated $250,000/year in blood acquisition costs/year (average savings over a 3-year period). Such programs are being successfully established in forward-thinking hospitals in the United States, Europe, and Canada, with several hospitals reporting dramatic changes in clinical practices and millions of dollars in savings. HOSPITAL has the opportunity to extend its reputation as a leader in PBM and transfusion safety by establishing the TSO position.

#### Problem Statement

Analysis of blood usage throughout HOSPITAL identified that a significant percentage of blood components were ordered outside of evidence-based guidelines or in excessive amounts, transfusion-related adverse events are underrecognized and underreported, and a significant amount of blood is discarded each year due to inefficient clinical practices (see below). However, currently there is no designated institutional

---

*This example is not meant to be an extensive business proposal template; rather, it is provided to serve as a reference for individuals desiring to create their own business proposal.

representative fully committed to the assurance of safety during transfusion, despite the recognition that significant safety and financial gaps continue to exist. An institutional transfusion gap analysis has revealed the following:

- *Transfusion ordering (safety/financial):* 38% of transfusion episodes did not meet hospital criteria at the time of the medical record review. In addition, 86% of Red Blood Cell (RBC) transfusions were ordered as 2+ unit orders, with only 14% single-unit RBC transfusion orders. This practice leads to excessive and often unnecessary transfusion exposure.
- *Adverse event recognition/reporting (safety):* There is a very low reported transfusion reaction rate (0.2%) compared with expected rates in the transfusion literature (>1.0%). In a recent audit, five transfusion reactions were identified that were either unrecognized or unreported by clinical staff—a situation that compromises patient safety.
- *Product waste/discard (financial):* Blood component wastage, mostly due to modifiable causes, cost the organization 1088 units of blood, or $100,000 in hospital costs for blood product discard.

**Proposed Solution**

It is proposed that a Transfusion Safety Officer position be created to support the PBM and transfusion safety initiative. This proposal aims at hiring a dedicated individual *(1 FTE)* to work closely with the Transfusion Service, Quality Department, and Blood Utilization Committee in order to accomplish the following goals: 1) Provide oversight and monitoring for transfusion ordering and blood administration practices; 2) Work through the appropriate peer review channels to generate feedback mechanisms to the staff and physicians of all hospital units; 3) Establish a nonpunitive mechanism for the reporting of errors and near-miss events during transfusions; 4) Provide ongoing education regarding transfusion practices; and 5) Progressively establish proactive hospital strategies to reduce the risk of transfusion in certain patient populations (eg, blood conservation strategies). This position would report directly to the HOSPITAL ADMINISTRATOR (eg, Chief Quality Officer, Transfusion Medicine Medical Director, Chief Medical Officer).

*Alternative Solution*

The goals above would remain the same; however, the dedicated role would be established as part-time (0.4-0.6 FTE). This would likely be a full-time hospital employee who could dedicate half of his or her time to PBM and transfusion safety (eg, Quality Department RN).

## Project Description

The TSO is expected to work outside the context of the blood bank to ensure coordination and integration among all hospital departments, service lines, and health-care professionals who play a role in managing blood component usage. The development of a TSO position is similar to that of other roles focused on improving patient safety such as medication safety officers. Similarly, the TSO's activities will involve education, coordination of direct observation audits, clinical consultation, tracking of data on key quality indicators, implementation of process improvement projects, and blood utilization review. This position will create hospital savings by reducing the unnecessary/inappropriate ordering of blood components, decreasing blood component wastage, and reducing patient adverse events during blood transfusion. The TSO's efforts will focus on establishing and sustaining the infrastructure behind a comprehensive PBM program.

### Reduce Blood Utilization

The TSO position has been shown in other programs to improve patient safety and increase efficiency and stewardship through reductions in unnecessary and excessive transfusion ordering practices. The TSO will support physician education efforts on evidence-based transfusion practice. This will be accomplished through the following: 1) coordination of PBM-related CME presentations for the medical staff (internal/external speakers); 2) dissemination of evidence-based references to the medical staff pertinent to their specialty; and 3) regular participation on physician committees to provide updates in PBM and transfusion safety. The TSO will also provide oversight and monitoring for transfusion ordering practices to evaluate transfusion practice (eg, transfusion audits, benchmarking, LIS reports). The TSO will be expected to work through the appropriate peer review channels to generate feedback mechanisms to the medical staff based on their transfusion practice.

    The TSO will also strive to establish proactive hospital strategies to reduce the risk of transfusion in certain patient populations. Possible strategies include anemia management, reducing hospital acquired anemia, cardiac surgery blood conservation, and perioperative blood conservation strategies. The PBM initiative is expected to reduce blood utilization 5% annually from baseline for the next 3 years. This will result in a blood acquisition savings of $125K in year 1, $250K savings in year 2, and $375K savings in year 3.

## Reduce Blood Component Wastage

In the past 12 months, over $100K in RBC, platelet, plasma, and Cryo-precipitated AHF units were wasted or discarded because of inefficient clinical practices. Therefore, the waste was mostly avoidable. The TSO will improve coordination, communication, and teamwork between the Transfusion Service and clinical departments to reduce the incidence of blood component mishandling and wastage. The investigation, intervention, and monitoring of improvements in blood unit handling will be a major focus of the TSO. Each year it is expected that a full-time TSO will be able to decrease blood component wastage by 10% ($10,000). A 30% reduction ($30,000) from baseline is anticipated by the end of year 3.

## Optimize Transfusion Safety

Hospital blood administration audits demonstrate significant clinical knowledge and performance gaps. Failure to address these issues increases the risk of transfusion errors, transfusion-related adverse events, and medicolegal liability for the hospital. As described above, the TSO's efforts are expected to reduce unnecessary and excessive blood component orders resulting in less overall risk for transfusion adverse events. However, the TSO will also strive to optimize the safety of the transfusion process for those patients who cannot avoid transfusion. This will be accomplished using a multi-modal strategy designed to educate clinicians on safe transfusion practice and providing regular oversight, monitoring, and feedback on clinical transfusion practices. The TSO will provide formal and informal education on transfusion safety and transfusion reactions for all clinicians involved in the transfusion process. These vehicles will include nursing orientation, unit-based in-service sessions, CME/CNE presentations, and needs-based presentations at physician and nursing committee meetings. Additional strategies will include regular auditing of clinical documentation related to the transfusion process and direct observations of blood administration to identify and address safety gaps in the process. The TSO will also review all transfusion-related adverse events and identify mechanisms to improve the recognition, reporting, and management of transfusion reactions.

Thus, the overall goal of the proposed Transfusion Safety Officer position is to make clinical care safer for the thousands of patients who receive transfusions at HOSPITAL every year while significantly reducing non-labor costs for HOSPITAL. The continued cost of not having a coordinating TSO will likely outweigh the funding or reallocation of resources needed to support a full-time TSO position. The cost of salary and benefits for the professional TSO position may be put into perspective by calculating the dollar amount per unit ordered or transfused in the institution.

## Financial Analysis

|  | Year 1 ($) | Year 2 ($) | Year 3 ($) |
| --- | --- | --- | --- |
| **Budget Category** | | | |
| Salary and benefits expenses | 100,000 | 105,000 | 110,000 |
| Hospital educational resources (guest speakers) | 10,000 | 7,500 | 5,000 |
| TSO educational resources (conference attendance) | 5,000 | 5,000 | 5,000 |
| Total annual operating expenses | 115,000 | 117,500 | 120,000 |
| **Potential Savings** | | | |
| Reduced blood utilization (5% year) | 125,000 | 250,000 | 375,000 |
| Reduced blood wastage (10% year) | 10,000 | 20,000 | 30,000 |
| Reduced transfusion costs (tubing, reagents, etc) | 15,000 | 30,000 | 45,000 |
| Total savings | 150,000 | 300,000 | 450,000 |
| **Return on Investment** | 35,000 | 182,500 | 330,000 |

## Conclusion and Recommendations

The atmosphere around PBM and transfusion safety is changing rapidly and there is now a national patient safety initiative around evidence-based, safe transfusion practices. In order to maintain our status as a national leader, HOSPITAL must establish a formal TSO position to implement and sustain a comprehensive PBM program. The results of this program will improve patient safety while significantly reducing non-labor costs. The estimated ROI for HOSPITAL is estimated at $547,500 over a 3-year period if the full-time TSO position is established.

In: Johnson ST, Puca KE, eds.
*Transfusion Medicine's Emerging Positions: Transfusion Safety
Officers and Patient Blood Management Coordinators*
Bethesda, MD: AABB Press, 2013

# 8

# *The Canadian Perspective: Optimizing Patient Care through Transfusion Safety*

SHELLEY FEENSTRA, RN, AND
CAROLE ANN LaGRANGE, MLT

 THE TAINTED BLOOD TURMOIL FACED BY THE CANA-
dian blood system in the late 1970s and 80s launched an
overwhelming cultural change and approach to transfusion
medicine in Canada. In 1997, with the release of the Royal
Commission of Inquiry Report on the Blood System[1] (Krever
Report), Canada began to rebuild and reform the national blood system.
Inspired by the report recommendations, government officials, clinical
practice leaders, and transfusion medicine experts recognized the neces-
sity to consult, collaborate, and focus on quality and transfusion safety—
effecting change to ensure optimal patient outcomes.

---

Shelley Feenstra, RN, TMS Clinical Resource Clinician, Transfusion Medicine Labora-
tory, Vancouver Coastal Health, Vancouver, British Columbia, and Carole Ann LaGrange,
MLT, Transfusion Medicine Safety Officer, Central Zone Laboratory Services, Alberta
Health Services, Red Deer, Alberta, Canada
The authors have disclosed no conflicts of interest.

## Overview

One of the cornerstones of Canada's nationally funded health-care system is public safety. Health-care policy and subsequently organizational practice models are guided by several key principles[2] that focus on the consumer or in the case of transfusion, the recipient. In Canada, blood safety is regulated by the federal government. To reduce risk and enhance safety of blood and blood components, all facilities that collect, store, process, and transfuse are required to meet applicable standards, some of which are subject to various levels of regulatory oversight.[3]

Canada's national blood system consists of two operators, Canadian Blood Services and Héma-Québec. Through their services all transfusion recipients have equal access to safe blood and blood components. After the Krever Report, transfusion medicine experts and government officials responded by developing strategies to minimize impact on the existing health-care system while expediting adoption of the report recommendations related to blood safety, accountability, financing, research and development, public confidence, and blood component utilization. As a result, several management models were developed and the framework and foundation for provincial blood safety programs evolved in Canada.

## The Transfusion Safety Officer

From a quality management perspective, the interface of laboratory and clinical transfusion practice is a point where transfusion medicine encounters significant challenges in achieving compliance with applicable standards to ensure product and patient safety. With the exception of a few, almost all quality systems essentials (QSEs) stretch beyond the walls of the laboratory into the clinical practice setting.

In Canada, the Province of Québec was first to establish the unique role of a transfusion safety officer (TSO). To improve safety and transparency, the provincial government created and funded clinical and laboratory TSO positions responsible for all aspects of transfusion quality and safety, under the direction of the transfusion medical director. These positions are held by either a registered nurse or a medical laboratory technologist. Depending on the size and level of activity of the facility, one or more TSOs may be responsible for the site. The Québec TSOs have created a provincial association to network with colleagues, standardize practices, promote competencies, and develop educational resources.

The Province of Ontario created the Ontario Transfusion Coordinators program (ONTraC),[4] a network of transfusion nurse coordinators who support a provincially designed program for both the patient and the health-care professionals to enhance awareness of and access to blood conservation measures. The results of this program have shown it to be efficient and cost effective, reducing transfusion adverse events and decreasing blood component utilization.

Throughout the other Canadian provinces, transfusion medicine leaders are actively seeking funding to establish, maintain, or sustain a TSO or equivalent-type position. Although limited in numbers, these leaders have had some success with health authority, provincial, or program-based funding and similar TSO positions have been created to integrate clinical and laboratory transfusion practice. Using their unique expertise and skill set, TSOs promote transfusion safety; guide, develop, and implement policies and procedures; provide education and communication resources; oversee surveillance and blood component utilization; and, thus, ultimately optimize safe patient care.

The Canadian Society for Transfusion Medicine (CSTM),[5] an organization that promotes excellence in transfusion medicine for Canadians in all provinces, promotes these emerging roles, and supports opportunities for education and networking. More significantly, CSTM established within their *Standards for Hospital Transfusion Services*,[6] the recognition that a transfusion service "should have a transfusion safety officer with defined and documented duties."

## TSO Roles and Responsibilities

The role of the TSO (or equivalent position) is to improve the quality and safety of transfusion practice. Although responsibilities are dependent on the scope of practice, skill set, and expertise of the individual TSO, it is important to establish consistent role expectations and competencies. As is often seen with TSO or equivalent positions, practice is built on a partnership between a clinical and a transfusion medicine laboratory specialist. An exhaustive list of verbs can be used to describe the responsibilities associated with achieving the simple, yet very broad definition of the TSO role. However, one key indicator for assurance that transfusion practices are compliant with the applicable standards to ensure quality and safety is accreditation. Even so, accreditation itself reflects only a snapshot in time. The basic requirements for laboratory accreditation are found in the core of a quality management system. In an effective quality management system, the validation process is ongoing and the job is never "done." The TSO may have some key responsibilities in part or all of the following QSEs:

1.  Organization
    *   Identify role and reporting lines on the organization chart.
    *   Develop job descriptions.[7]
    *   Lead or participate in transfusion committee activities.
    *   Communicate information related to transfusion safety to health-care professionals.
    *   Facilitate multilevel policy and processes (ie, informed consent, recipient notification).
    *   Participate in developing policies (ie, disaster planning, recipient notification).

2.  Personnel
    *   Develop and maintain a formal competency training program.
    *   Provide initial training/orientation for staff involved in blood-related activities.
    *   Ensure ongoing competency assessment of staff.
    *   Evaluate education or training opportunities.

3.  Equipment
    *   Ensure that procedures exist for validation, calibration, and preventive maintenance of equipment.
    *   Troubleshoot as required to ensure the safety of the blood component or recipient.
    *   Ensure that policies, procedures, and training are in place (ie, clinical sample collection, packaging of emergency red cells, obtaining products in the absence of the laboratory personnel) where transfer of function occurs.
    *   Facilitate compliance with blood product storage policies.
    *   Assist with policies, processes, and procedures for use and quality assurance of processing and administration equipment (ie, blood warmers, infusion devices).
    *   Consult with biomedical staff as required.

4.  Purchasing and Inventory
    *   Participate in formal Request for Proposal processes and equipment evaluation.
    *   Liaise with contract suppliers.
    *   Review and evaluate contracts and suppliers as required.

5.  Process Control
    *   Review literature (research, published guidelines, standards on blood use and indications, blood transfusion techniques, alter-

natives to blood transfusion and effects of transfusion) and make applicable recommendations.
- Assist with defining the processes related to:
  - Product ordering (ie, order entry, preprinted orders).
  - Product receipt, storage, traceability, and final disposition.
  - Sample collection, receipt, and documentation evaluation.
  - Recipient identification and alternative processes.
  - Emergency transfusion.
  - Prenatal testing and sample (cord and blood) collection.
  - Component modification and usage guidelines.
  - Transportation of products between sites.
  - Issuing of blood, visual inspection, records.
  - Transfusion administration and documentation, including neonatal transfusions.
  - Perioperative blood conservation, (ie, preoperative assessment or blood recovery).
  - Home infusion/transfusion.
6. Documents and Records
  - Ensure procedures are available, current, compliant, and accessible to the staff.
  - Develop documentation and tracking process for training (see Figure 8-1).
  - Define policies for document retention.
  - Maintain audit records.
  - Advise, review, and revise documentation format, control, and archiving to ensure compliance with applicable blood standards.
7. Information Management
  - Liaise with external programs (ie, home infusion programs or public health).
  - Liaise with blood supplier, accrediting/inspection agency, nurses, physicians, and allied health-care professionals.
  - Oversee the completion of look-back, trace-back, withdrawals, and recalls initiated by blood operators.
  - Respond to patient inquiries associated with blood transfusion.
  - Develop process for recipient notification.
  - Develop reports for the transfusion committee.
8. Non-conformance Event Management
  - Participate in adverse event investigation, root-cause analysis.
  - Complete reports (ie, error management system).
  - Create reports for medical director and/or transfusion committee, assess for trends.

**Training and Competency - Template for TSO**

TSO Name: _____

Site: _____

Date ___/___/___

**QSE: Process Improvement**

| Responsibility: | Date(s) completed | Strengths / strengths to build on /feedback | TSO Initials | Review Required dd /mm /yy |
|---|---|---|---|---|
| Prepare for and participate in : | | | | |
| Regional orientation of RN's performing transfusions | | | | |
| Unit-based in-service session specific to: | | | | |
| 1. Adverse events/ incidents<br>2. Transfusion reactions<br>3. New processes/technology/products | | | | |
| Training and auditing of inter- and intra-hospital transport of blood | | | | |
| Key stakeholder committees, representing transfusion medicine | | | | |

Trainer _____

Signature _____ Date ___/___/___

Print name _____

Figure 8- 1. Training and competency template for transfusion safety officers.[7]

- Review and complete transfusion reaction investigation (ie, maintain data base, follow up with blood supplier, Public Health Agency of Canada, and/or manufacturers as applicable).
9. Assessments
   - Facilitate process for self-assessments.
   - Participate in the development of key quality indicators.
   - Develop audit tools.
   - Participate in inspection/accreditation by provincial agencies and/or AABB and College of American Pathologists (CAP).
10. Process Improvement
    - Conduct internal audits such as:
      - Blood component utilization, recipient notification.
      - Data analysis, trending, and forecasting.
      - Bedside (ie, documentation, informed consent).
      - Retrospective audits (ie, wasted/discarded product, massive transfusion review).
    - Participate in external audits such as:
      - Proficiency surveys.
      - Promoting corrective action that is educational not punitive.
      - Reporting to quality assurance and quality improvement committees at regular intervals.
    - Facilitate transfusion education: Conducting in-service sessions and provision of resource material for nursing, medical staff, and allied health-care professionals. This could include:
      - Participation in orientation for newly hired staff.
      - In-service sessions specific to adverse events including errors, incidents, and transfusion reactions.
      - Introduction of new products, technology, or processes.
      - Training or in-service sessions for staff involved in intra- and inter-hospital transport of blood.
      - Participation on committees that require transfusion medicine input.
11. Customer Service
    - Develop and execute service satisfaction surveys (ie, patients, physicians, employees, peers).
    - Measure feedback and engage stakeholders in process improvement.
12. Facility and Safety
    - Coordinate with stakeholders in emergency response/disaster and blood shortage contingency planning.

## Training/Skill Set

Opportunities and resources are available to assist the registered nurse or medical laboratory technologist to advance their level of knowledge and scope of practice to become a TSO. Complex patients require complex care; there is nothing simple or basic about transfusion medicine or the patient requiring transfusion. The skills can be acquired, the learning is life-long, and expertise should be considered a goal.

Learning opportunities can be simple: review literature, ask questions, attend in-service sessions, e-learning, online webinars, conferences, and observation time on the bench. Or the opportunities may be complex: establish a care plan for a chronically transfused patient, suggest alternatives, implement massive transfusion protocols, or provide leadership and direction if and when an error occurs.

The registered nurse TSO possesses the knowledge, skills, attitude, and judgment to transfuse safely using the "Nine Rights of Safe Transfusion": Right indication, order, sample, patient, product, dose, time, route, and documentation (see Appendix 8-1). The medical laboratory technologist TSO possesses the knowledge to perform complex serologic testing, present critical information, and, most important, provide the patient with the most appropriate treatment—whether that involves transfusion or the avoidance of transfusion in favor of pharmacologic, blood recovery, or other strategies. TSOs with either background should acknowledge and respect their working partnership and each other's role in supporting and promoting vein-to-vein safety. The decisions related to transfusion remain the responsibility of the medical health-care provider.

The registered nurse TSO must develop a working knowledge of blood banking theories, application of the *CSTM Standards*, and the purpose and structure of a quality management system. The medical laboratory technologist TSO should establish a working relationship with colleagues in clinical practice, become fluent with medical indications for transfusion, learn to apply the Nine Rights of Safe Transfusion, and understand the clinical techniques and procedures involved in transfusing the patient.

## Future Expectations

Transfusion safety officer (or equivalent) positions have revolutionized the approach to the quality and safety of transfusion practice in Canada.

However, challenges remain. Health-care budgets, human resources, expertise, and role clarity will always be factors in establishing and sustaining these new and successful roles and programs. Establishing a regional, provincial, and national network of TSOs will facilitate communication of best practices, thus optimizing patient care and enhancing institutional efficiencies.

## Acknowledgments

The authors thank their colleagues Kieran Biggins, RT, FIMLS; Marilyn Collins, MLT, ART; John Freedman, MD, FRCPC; Ana Lima, RN, HP(ASCP); Heather Panchuk, MLT; and Bonnie Selcer, RN, for their support.

## References

1. Royal Commission of Inquiry Report on the Blood System in Canada. Ottawa, Canada: Government of Canada Publications, 1997. [Available at http://publica tions.gc.ca/site/eng/72717/publication.html (accessed August 27, 2013).]
2. Mission statement. Ottawa, Canada: Canadian Public Health Association, 2013. [Available at http://www.cpha.ca/en/about.aspx (accessed August 27, 2013).]
3. Fact sheet: Canada's blood regulations. Ottawa, Canada: Health Canada, 2013. [Available at http://www.hc-sc.gc.ca/dhp-mps/brgtherap/activit/fs-fi/cbr-rcs-reg-eng.php (accessed August 27, 2013).]
4. ONTraC program information. Toronto, Canada: Ontario Nurse Transfusion Coordinators, 2013. [Available at http://www.ontracprogram.com/home-program-ontrac.aspx (accessed August 27, 2013).]
5. CSTM mission and value statement. Markham, Canada: Canadian Society for Transfusion Medicine, 2013. [Available at http://www.transfusion.ca/en (accessed August 27, 2013).]
6. Standards for hospital transfusion services, version 3. Markham, Canada: Canadian Society for Transfusion Medicine, 2011:2.5.
7. TSO job descriptions. Markham, Canada: Canada's Transfusion Safety Officers, 2013. [Available at http://www.transfusionsafety.ca/about-tso.html (accessed August 27, 2013).]

## Appendix 8-1. Nine Rights of Transfusion Administration*

Transfusion Safety - How many "Rights" are there to consider when developing "best practice" training materials?

Many of the registered nurses practicing today were trained on the "5 Rights" of safe medication administration, which included right patient, medication, dose, time, and route. In the last decade or so, those "5 rights" transitioned into "7" as right indication and documentation were added to the list.

However, when it comes to blood administration, one of the initial steps in the transfusion process is #8, "right sample" for the group and screen testing. It is crucial that a link exists between the sample, the patient, and the product administered; usually this is in the form of an identification band. This is a pretty simple concept to those who are familiar with all the processes involved in the provision of a safe product for transfusion.

The lack of an identification band at the time of transfusion is a "red flag" for a potential error. It is one of those "missed opportunities" frequently mentioned when an adverse event or near-miss involves wrong patient identification. This is an opportunity for teaching and increasing clinical awareness surrounding the safety component of patient identification. The lack of an identification band at the time of transfusion may indicate that key steps related to confirming and verifying the patient identification were incomplete at the time of sample collection. Absence of the band can plant a "seed of caution" for the clinician and prompt consultation with the transfusion service. Once the concept is understood, replacing the armband is no longer an acceptable option for the prudent transfusionist.

In addition, when multiple blood components are required, the physician's orders should reflect the sequence in which the components should be administered based on the clinical indication and availability. "Right product sequence" brings the list to *at least* "Nine" rights to teach clinicians in relation to best practices in transfusion administration.

---

*Used with permission from Feenstra S. Transfusion safety tips. CSTM Bulletin 2009;21 (3):72.

# Index